Where The Action Is

A B_____/Mark

G/L
REGAL
BOOKS

A BIBLE
COMMENTARY
FOR LAYMEN

**A Division of G/L Publications
Glendale, California, U.S.A.**

These pages are fondly and gratefully
dedicated to the Adult Bible Class
at Eagle Rock Covenant Church,
Los Angeles, California,
whose teacher has learned so much from them.

Other good Regal reading on related subjects:
    Alexander, David S., *The New Testament in Living Pictures.*
    Barnhouse, Donald Gray, *The Love Life.*
    La Sor, William S., *Men Who Knew Christ.*
    Mears, Henrietta C., *A Look at the New Testament.*
    Mears, Henrietta C., *What the Bible Is All About.*
    Palau, Luis, *Walk on Water, Pete.*
    Stott, John R.W., *Understanding the Bible.*
    Vigeveno, H.S., *Jesus the Revolutionary.*
    Vigeveno, H.S., *13 Men Who Changed the World.*

The Scripture quotations in *Where the Action Is* are
the author's own translation except where noted.
Other versions used are:
The Revised Standard Version of the Bible, copyrighted
1946 and 1952 by the Division of Christian Education
of the NCCC, U.S.A., and used by permission.
The King James Version.
The American Standard Version, 1901.
The Moffatt Translation.
The New International Version, New Testament.
Copyright © 1973 by New York Bible Society
International. Used by permission.

Third Printing, 1978

Published by
Regal Books Division, G/L Publications
Glendale, California 91209
Printed in U.S.A.

Library of Congress Catalog Card No. 75-23515
ISBN 0-8307-0361-6

 # Contents

A Teacher's Manual and Student Discovery Guide,
for Bible Study groups using *Where the Action Is*,
are available from your church supplier.

 **Preface**

On the same day as this preface is being written I came across an article in a Christian weekly paper that took me by surprise, to put it mildly. The writer's suggestion was that, since there is a shortage of almost everything we use today, and since this applies to time and energy, those who want to break out in print should think twice before doing so. Are they putting their time and effort to best use? And are they simply going over old ground and rehashing other people's ideas in their latest volumes? And, aren't there too many books in the stores in any case? Why add to the list?

Now, he has a point. I wouldn't for a moment deny that there are probably too many books on the market, and that there is always the danger of overlapping and becoming redundant. So, why yet another book on the Gospels? And Mark's Gospel in particular?

Let the reader decide if this book was worth writing and worth reading. I can only respond that it has helped me to put some orderly thoughts on paper and to offer them to a wider public.

The Gospel of Mark is one of the great books of all time. As far as we can tell, *it is the first Christian book about Jesus Christ to be written and circulated.* With Mark's effort, as the Spirit directed him, Christianity went into the publishing business. True, Paul's letters were earlier, but these were occasional documents, mainly addressed to some local congregations. This Gospel was written for Christians in Rome, but it is obviously intended for a more extensive class of readers, namely Christians in the Roman Empire across the Mediterranean world.

I believe that any help we can get to assist our understanding of Mark and his Gospel is good. Even better if we come to have a clearer picture of Jesus Christ through a reading of this Gospel. For it is true, as Laurence Housman has said, that the Church owes so much to John Mark—

The saint who first found grace to pen
The life which was the Life of men.

We owe so much to the first of our written Gospels. That's why we read it today. That's why books will continue to be written about this Gospel. Suppose Mark himself had felt that it wasn't worth it—to write and to publish his story of Jesus. How much poorer would we all be?

My thanks to several classes of men and women, at seminary and church, who heard lectures based on these materials, and to Mrs. Ann Lausch who expertly transcribed the manuscript and made it presentable.

Ralph P. Martin
Fuller Theological Seminary
Pasadena, California

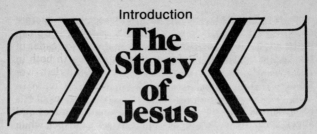

The Story of Jesus

As Told by Mark

The Gospel according to Mark holds a cherished place in the interest of the Bible-reading public. Young Christians especially are encouraged to read it because (it is promised) its language is clear, its narrative of Jesus' life swift-flowing and entertaining, and its appeal to the non-theological mind is direct. The inference is that all readers appreciate a biography simply told. Mark's Gospel is a good story, told with an economy of words and a forthrightness of style. Therefore, Mark's Gospel tops the charts in the popular ratings.

To a large measure this is true. No one can deny that there *is* an immediate appeal about this Gospel and that its message strikes home to us, living as we do in a world in which we want quick answers to deep questions, a religious book which we can read in haste (if not in a hurry) and a story of a human life with which we can identify. A generation which gets action-packed drama on the TV news with on-the-spot coverage and instant news analysis is bound to be drawn to this Gospel—if it is drawn to any of the Church's holy books. This is simply because Mark's Gospel is full of activity, rich in dramatic quality, and centers on a heroic figure whose mastermind controls the movement of the plot. Talking is not much in His line (in this Gospel); He strides across the chapters with a singleness of purpose and a magnetic appeal to others which identifies Him as a Leader with obvious charisma.

It is an easy step from this impression to go on to conclude that Mark's Gospel appeals to us because its picture of Jesus is manageable and fits into a framework we can understand. He appears (so it seems to the rapid reader of the Gospel) essentially human and down-to-earth both in His attitudes and His actions. We are not puzzled over stories of His marvelous birth, for Mark plunges immediately into His adult life. Equally there are no stories of His resurrection, with dead men getting up out of graves and angels speaking to distraught women. Mark's Gospel, while it does proclaim the essential truth that He is risen (16:6), speaks of the messenger as a young man and then dramatically breaks off with the flight of the women from the tomb in great fear—a natural reaction, to be sure (16:8).

Many features of the Markan narrative are added to make up a picture of the human figure of Jesus. This evangelist does not balk at recording items of information or narrating the stories of Jesus which present Jesus in very human light. We shall study these features in some detail. But we shall also see ample evidence for believing that this impression of a simple Galilean peasant-teacher is only part of Mark's material. Interwoven with the fabric is the apparently contrasting pattern of the enigmatic figure of the strong Son of God; the strong man who shackles Satan and neutralizes his power in order to expel the demons and release the captives; the miracle-worker whose power extends over turbulent nature (4:35–41) as well as distracted human nature; the imperious kingly figure who exercises authority as Son of man on earth and will be the final arbiter of men's destiny (8:38); and the King of Israel who entered upon His rule by the way of the cross.

Jesus in Mark's Gospel is fully human and strangely and insistently authoritative, with a power at work in Him that none but God can claim. This story is, above all else, a record of activity, and Mark has us almost out of breath in following the movements and entering into the experiences of Jesus and His friends. This Gospel is full of action. It is "where the action is," and it calls us to share it with the Lord and His disciples.

7

1
It Began in Galilee

Mark 1:1—3:6

WHERE ARE WE GOING?

Pilate, the Roman civil servant in Palestine, was caught in a difficult situation. He had before his bench where he acted as magistrate an accused person who was evidently a center of controversy. That person was guilty of no social crime, and anyone less likely to lead a revolt against Rome's mighty empire is hard to imagine. But the Jewish leaders hated this prisoner, called Jesus.

Why was it? Pilate mused. All they could say about Him was that He excited the people with His teaching—and then, in a phrase which sticks in the mind—they went on, 'He started from Galilee, and now he is here' (Luke 23:5, *Moffatt*). Jesus had started something they didn't like, but they couldn't deny its force. He had begun to teach in Galilee; now He was in Jerusalem. Pilate had to make up his mind what to do with Jesus.

8

And so did everyone else in Mark—disciples, tax collectors, Pharisees, the sick and demon possessed, family and friends—every person whose life touched His. As confrontation after confrontation passes before our eyes, and as we see Jesus healing, teaching, praying, making disciples, one goal remains uppermost in the mind of the writer —that each reader, whether in the first century or the twentieth, should make up his mind about Jesus. There is no avoiding this decision. Pilate's dilemma is really the ground plan and theme of the Gospel of Mark.

WHAT DOES IT SAY?

Mark's Gospel was very probably the first of the Gospels to be written, in the middle of the '60s, and it comes to us, so Christians have believed, with Peter's authority behind it. The hand that wrote it is Mark's but the voice is the voice of Peter who looked on John Mark as "my son" (1 Pet. 5:13).

John Mark is no stranger either. He was well known in the early church in several ways. His mother kept a house in Jerusalem (Acts 12:12) which became a regular gathering place for Christians. John Mark accompanied Paul on his first missionary journey (Act 13:5). When the unfortunate incident of his returning home occurred (Acts 13:13; 15:37–39), it led him to join forces with his cousin Barnabas (Col. 4:10). Then later, although he was reconciled to Paul (2 Tim. 4:11), who pays him a magnificent compliment, he attached himself to Peter, while at the same time in his life he spent a period in the company of Paul in his prison (Philem. 24). In all, we can see how well he knew the leading apostolic figures in his day. He was therefore well equipped to compose the story of Jesus.

Mark's Title Page/1:1

Later on, we shall see how the points Mark emphasizes in his Gospel-book fit into a situation in the early church where these emphases are needed. For the present, we focus on one item, and what is more natural than to take a look at the title page of a book we are reading if we want to know what it is all about? The title of Mark's Gospel is in his opening verse: "The beginning of the gospel of Jesus Christ, the Son of God" (1:1, *RSV*). This one text tells us several things.

1. Mark's story is ready to begin. So he entitles this book "The beginning," perhaps in a conscious recall of Genesis 1:1, "In the beginning God created." So *there is a new start in the world's history about to be made.* God is at work in His Son—and this should be a time of rejoicing as at the first creation when all the sons of God shouted for joy (Job 38:7).

2. The book proclaims good news—"The beginning of the gospel . . ." *Gospel,* meaning "good news," was a common term in Mark's contemporary world for a "historical event which introduces a new situation for the world"[1] such as the enthronement of the Roman emperor. Augustus' birthday is hailed in a well-known inscription from Priene on the Asia Minor coast (dated 9 B.C.) as "the beginning of joyful news (*euangelion,* the same word as in Mark's verse) for the world." Roman readers of the Gospel record would immediately recognize the term.

The gospel in Mark is the good news that Jesus brought into the world, and that news centers in Him, for *He is the gospel.*

When the first believers were in debate with adherents of other religions in the Roman Empire, the question was asked of them: What new thing is there in your religion? What is different about your faith? They gave a fine response. The new thing that Jesus Christ brought into the world was *Himself.*

Mark will set down the good news in telling the life of Jesus, whose story-line is that the time of God's purpose is now fulfilled. The Kingdom of God, His rule over the world and human lives, is about to exert its influence. Wake up to this reality, proclaims Mark, and put your trust in the good news which Jesus brought and embodied (Mark 1:14, 15).

3. "The beginning of the gospel of Jesus Christ, *the Son of God.*" Who is this Jesus? Mark's title picks up the Chris-

tian creed and boldly asserts, He is the Son of God. You will find this description of Jesus running through the 16 chapters of Mark like a silver thread (1:1,11; 3:11; 8:38; 9:7; 12:6; 13:32; 14:61; 15:39). Because he is focusing on Jesus as the Son of God, Mark has no apparent interest in Jesus' background and birth. Mary, His human mother, is mentioned only indirectly (6:3), though we do learn that Jesus spent His youthful years as a carpenter at Nazareth. Rather than trace His boyhood and early manhood, this evangelist makes Jesus suddenly burst on to the scene.

A Messenger in the Wilderness/1:2–8

True, the ground is prepared for His appearance in the ministry of John the Baptist (1:2–8), who sets the people's expectation astir with his announcement that a great one, more-than-a-prophet, a Bearer of the Holy Spirit, is soon to be seen. John plays the role of Elijah, both in dress and diet in the desert (see 2 Kings 1:8) and, for Jews well-versed in the Old Testament, the next person to come after Elijah's return is God! (see Mal. 4:5; Mark 9:9–13).

In verses 2 and 3, "Isaiah the prophet" is the authority given for Mark's introduction of John as the herald of the Lord. These verses include parts of Malachi 3:1; 4:5; Exodus 23:20, as well as Isaiah 40:3. Possibly Isaiah is mentioned as the best-known part of the Old Testament that is quoted or as the title of this section of a Christian book of Old Testament "testimonies" to Christ, prepared for apologetic use.

John comes fulfilling two prophecies: (1) he is the "messenger" promised by God as the forerunner of the Messiah, and (2) he appeared "in the wilderness," where divine revelation was expected. John is thus the "prophesied preparer,"[2] and well qualified to make ready for Jesus' coming.

"The wilderness" (v. 4) is the Jordan valley. John is known by a characteristic activity: he baptized his fellow-Jews in anticipation of the coming of God's rule. In this way he fulfilled the hope of a faithful "prophet" who would appear in the last days (see Deut. 18:15–19). The preaching of John called for repentance. That is, he summoned his

11

hearers to a radical change in their way of living. The accompanying promise was the offer of forgiveness from God. In all he was seeking to make ready a people who should greet the deliverer, spoken of in verses 7,8.

The Son of God Baptized/1:9–11

Now let's take a look at 1:9–13 to see what happens to the Son of God as He begins His life's work on earth. At His baptism the sky is split open (a sign of God's coming down, Isa. 64:1). The Spirit, who had brooded over the old creation in the beginning (Gen. 1:2), descends in dove-like form. The Father's voice echoes loud and clear: "You are my dear and only Son. I have just set my favor upon you." Again, the attentive reader of this account, with the Old Testament in mind, would recall God's promise to crown His Messiah-Son as king (Ps. 2:6,7) and to commission by His Spirit His servant to carry out His purpose in the world (Isa. 42:1). If the reader dug a little deeper, he might see the parallel between Jesus the beloved Son of the Father and Isaac whom Abraham dearly loved (Gen. 22:2) and whose obedience to the patriarch's desires was such that he was willing to die.

There is a cluster of images here, all proclaiming who Jesus is: He is God's Son who is destined to reign as the king in the divine kingdom; He is Isaiah's suffering servant, endowed with the Spirit as the Lord's anointed one (Acts 10:38); He is the obedient son, ready to die because He loves God's will above all else.

The Son of God Tested/1:12,13

And He is the new Adam, tempted yet victorious (Mark 1:12,13). The wilderness is the scene of this testing, as it was for the Jews in the Old Testament. (See Ps. 95:7–11; Heb. 3:7–19.) "Forty days" reminds us of Moses on the mountain (Exod. 24:18) and Elijah's sojourn en route to Mount Horeb (1 Kings 19:8,15). Both Old Testament characters reappear in Mark 9:4,5.

But no conclusion of Jesus' temptation is given in this Gospel, nor are the details spelled out, as in Matthew 4:1–

11; Luke 4:1–13. The reason seems to be that for Mark the Lord's temptations extended throughout the entire course of His ministry, and that Mark's record explains the whole of Jesus' life as a facing of temptation and victory over it. The contest with Satan reappears in the healing miracles (3:20–29) and even in the debates with the Jewish leaders.[3]

In a sense, "the whole Gospel is an explanation of how Jesus was tempted."[4]

Two other brief comments about Jesus as the new Adam are included here. "He was with the wild animals" (v. 13). The first Adam was also a companion of wild animals (Gen. 2:19,20) to indicate the sign of a new age, one day to be realized on earth (Isa. 11:6–9) "And angels attended him" (Mark 1:13). Hebrews 1:6 tells us that, as the new Man, Jesus is to be worshiped by all the angels, over whom He is Lord (see also Heb. 2:5–9). Creation on all levels is aware of the presence of, and the identity of, the Son of God.

John's arrest, as a prisoner of Herod Antipas, tetrarch of Galilee (see Mark 6:14–29), is given as the historical event which prompted Jesus to begin His public preaching. Possibly Mark intends the reader to see John's being "handed over" (the Greek can mean both "arrest" and "delivered over") as a sign that God is at work, even in the evil designs of men. John's destiny foreshadows the destiny reserved for Jesus. The "Son of man" will end His days like John and be consigned to a "fate" which will be violent and evil (see 14:21).

Evidences of Jesus' True Identity/1:14–45

Jesus' first preaching (1:15) picks up Mark's chief interest, which is to show how the good news of God centers in Jesus, who announces the arrival of God's rule among men. "The time"—the critical moment in the world's history—is now; God's gracious rule is being established. The call is to get ready for it, and to welcome what God is beginning to do in the coming of His Son and Israel's Saviour.

Jesus' actions in this opening chapter clearly indicate that He is claiming to be God's personal agent. Let us set down the various ways these claims are made:

1. He calls men to His service (1:16–20) in a way that God summons His people to obey His commands (1 Kings 18:21). The call of the four disciples has been studied by recent writers and its significance drawn out.[5] It looks forward to the call of the Twelve (Mark 3:13–19) and their later mission (6:7–13,30). But it points ahead to what Jesus had in mind for these men from the beginning—that they should continue the work He was beginning and would later consummate by His sacrifice and victory over death (see 14:28; 16:7). Already Jesus gives the promise in this section: "I will make you become fishers of men."

The passage is also significant in showing that Jesus intended to form a company of followers who should share the work of the Kingdom with Him. Possibly this idea of a leader and a group is implied in His chosen title, "Son of man," found 14 times in this Gospel. Jesus was no solo performer or wandering itinerant preacher who worked on His own. He called men to be His helpers.

2. He teaches with firsthand authority (1:21,22) and overthrows the power of the demonic world which recognizes in Him its true master (1:23–28).

What arrested people's attention was the note of authority in Jesus' public teaching. The issue is neatly expressed in a contrast between the Jewish scribes—the theologians of the day—and Jesus: they taught with the authorities; He taught with authority. They based their opinions on previous decisions taken by the rabbis, and cited precedents in support. Jesus never deferred to any human "authority," but spoke directly out of His understanding of God's will which He, as divine Son, either knew intuitively or found in the Hebrew Bible. (For an example of this contrast which led to a head-on collision, see Mark 7:9–13.)

Jesus' teaching also got results, as when He exorcised the unclean spirit and restored mental and spiritual health to the sadly possessed man. It is little wonder the crowd was impressed (v. 27), and Jesus' fame spread (v. 28).

After leaving the synagogue and healing Peter's mother-in-law, Jesus ministered to many others in Capernaum who needed His touch.

In verses 32 and 33, Mark distinguishes between the sick and the demon possessed. For Jesus these unfortunate folk represented a crying human need, and He met both types of mental and physical disorder with compassion and powerful aid.

Early the next morning, He got up, and went out of the house to pray, only to be interrupted by Peter's frantic cry, "Everyone is searching for you" (v. 37). Probably we should see here a subtle temptation presented to Jesus by Peter's request. Wherever the verb "search" is found in Mark's Gospel, it is used either with a plainly hostile reference of Jesus' enemies seeking to arrest and kill Him (11:18; 12:12; 14:1,11,55), or in the bad sense of attempting to distract Jesus from His true mission (3:32; 8:11). Peter here, as often, is the mouthpiece of the temptation (see 8:33) and his approach to Jesus at prayer suggests that this advice in a Galilean town is part of a satanic temptation to confine Jesus' ministry to a settled place.

Jesus' reply is a rebuke, and He is concerned to move on in response to His wider mission (v. 38). "For that is why I came out" (v. 38) from Capernaum, or just possibly, "on my mission from God."

3. A leper is cleansed (1:40–45)—an impossible task, say the Jews of old, which only God can do. But Jesus does it!

"Moved with pity" (1:41), Jesus reached out His hand and touched the sick man. A variant reading in the Greek text suggests the words "moved with anger" instead of "moved with pity."[6] This is supported by the textual evidence and probably should be accepted as "an expression of righteous indignation [on the part of Jesus] at the ravages of sin, disease and death which take their toll even upon the living, a toll particularly evident in the leper."[7]

In cleansing the leper, Jesus accomplished a feat that illustrates His gracious concern to restore physical wholeness. "Leprosy" is a general term to cover a variety of chronic skin diseases and disfigurements. The story implies His criticism of the priesthood, who were powerless to help this unfortunate man. According to Leviticus 13 and 14, the priests had the sole power to make pronouncements on the cleansing of leprosy. Jesus, in verse 44, sends the cleansed leper back into society as a living witness whose new life incriminates the Judaic priesthood as impotent to assist. The man's cure is "a witness against" the priests, not the people.

The Growing Controversy with Judaism/2:1—3:6

The healing of the paralytic brings to the surface the controversy with official Judaism. The question of the debate in this story turns on verse 9: "Which is easier: to say to the paralytic, 'Your sins are forgiven' or to say, 'Get up, take your mat and walk'?" Both declarations of healing and forgiveness are easy to *say*—and equally difficult to accomplish.

Jesus then proceeds to criticize His adversaries who raise objection to His ministry: "You have nothing to say to either his moral or physical condition: I have both the solving word *and* the effective help." But the really criminal offense in the eyes of the rabbis was that Jesus Himself pronounced forgiveness, thus usurping a prerogative which belonged exclusively to God (see John 5:18 in the context of John 5:1–16).

The call to Levi the tax official (2:14) is inserted in a group of stories which show the developing controversy between Jesus and His opponents. There are five issues where the debate settles.

1. He claimed to forgive sins (2:5), and drew out the murmured comment: Why does this man talk like this? Who can forgive sins except God Himself?

2. He chose to consort with tax collectors and other bad company (2:13–17), treated by the Pharisees as beyond the pale of true religion, "people of the land," for whom no hope of salvation was possible (Luke 15:1; John 7:49). Further, He even called one of them to be His disciple. The position of tax collector in Roman-occupied Palestine was particularly obnoxious to the loyal Jews, smacking of compromise with the hated invaders and affording an opportunity for extortion and fraud (see Luke 19:1–10).

3. The fact that His disciples did not fast aroused serious

16

questioning (2:18–22). The immediate background here is the Jewish picture of fasting as a preparation for the coming of the Messiah. Jesus, in refusing to fast and to commit His followers to this practice, was tacitly announcing that the messianic age had already begun. The feast is now to be enjoyed and everyone is to be happy. But He is under no illusion that everyone shares that joy, and darkly hints that an ominous future will await Him and His disciples (2:20). God's Kingdom and official Judaism are scarcely compatible. They must affect each other, either by way of Jesus' revitalizing Judaism or (more probably) a distinct break and a new beginning. "New wine" calls for fresh wineskins (v. 22).

4. Jesus' Sabbath violations offended the Jews (2:23–28) who treated His disciples' practice of plucking the ears of corn as falling within the category of "reaping and threshing," one of the 39 schedules of work forbidden in Mishnah, a Jewish sourcebook of rabbinic comments on the law. The Master counters this objection with the assertion that the claims of the ministry override the Sabbath rules, and even the venerable Sabbath day (believed by the rabbis to antedate creation) is to give place to the Son of man, i.e., Jesus and His followers, in the exercise of the work of the Kingdom.

5. A further case of Sabbath breaking—the man with the withered hand restored—brings this series of conflict-stories to a close (3:1–6); yet the notice of verse 6 points unmistakably to the way in which the future will be shaped.

Mark 3:6 is a suitable point to sum up. Already we are faced with a big question: Who is this Jesus? He is a man, but so much more. He has made many friends and followers. But also He has enemies. What will the end of Him be?

WHAT DOES IT MEAN TODAY?

The leading theme in this opening section of the Gospel is the person of Jesus Christ and His claims. Without much by way of introduction we are faced with the figure of this charismatic prophet, teacher, healer, and leader of men. All of this is designed to force us to ask ourselves, Who is this?

17

He has shown His magnetic power in calling burly fishermen from their trade, and at least one professional man from his desk job. He has gained a tremendous fame in Galilee by healing the sick, actually touching the leprous man, and teaching in a way that the hearers could understand. There are no difficult concepts or mouth-filling technicalities. Just straight-from-the-shoulder plain speech —and He is saying things the authorities don't want to hear. He claims to do what only God can do. He overrides the respected but man-made regulations by which the law of Moses was hedged about, for He heals, and takes a meal in the cornfield, on the Sabbath. Best of all, where there is human need and distress, He is quick to respond. No "religious" restriction can stand in the way of His reaching out to help in God's name.

Well, this *is* a terrific introduction to Jesus, and we are looking at some big claims He is making for Himself and His teaching. The application might well follow through on some of these.

1. Jesus first came on to the scene as the perfect model of what God intends men and women to be. Read again 1:9–13. Jesus pleases His Father who loves Him. He is put to the test—compelled by the Spirit and assaulted by the enemy. Yet He is master, and even the wild beasts recognize the new Adam, as well as do the angels. Here is a picture of true manhood at its highest and holiest: loved by God, obedient to God, responsive to His mind, victorious over evil, as Jesus' Spirit controls His bodily appetites, and not the other way round. He is at peace with nature, and the steward of God's creation.

How far do I see myself in these descriptions? Have I risen to my "full stature" of personhood in Christ? Isn't this what Paul means in Ephesians 4:13 and Romans 8:29?

2. What was there about Jesus that made rough and tough men like Simon and Andrew leave all to follow him? Read again 1:16–20. Was this their first meeting with Jesus? (See John 1:35–42.)

Even if it wasn't, something of Jesus' irresistible appeal shines out of His simple call, "Follow me." How far am I willing to hear that voice and obey it at whatever cost? What sort of call from God would lead me to give up my job and launch out in an unknown adventure—with Jesus?

3. Strength and compassion in Jesus go together. He can be courageous in opposing the legalistic, unbending Jewish leaders (2:1–12; 3:6). Yet He is tender and gracious to reach out to human needs (1:29–31; 3:1–5). Where do I put the emphasis in character-building in my life? Am I strong in attacking evil things and am I being bold for what I believe to be the right thing, yet at the same time alert to needs around me and compassionate to men and women who are looking to me for assistance, encouragement, and the healing, supporting hand?

The hands of Jesus play a significant role in this Gospel (1:31; 5:41; 6:2; 7:33; 8:23; 9:27; 10:16). Who is it I can touch today?

4. These stories in chapters 1—3 pose a real problem in the area of organized religion and the freedom of the Spirit. There have to be rules and guidelines in the Christian church, just as there were laws to safeguard the Sabbath and rules about ceremonial uncleanness in the Judaism of Jesus' day. But what had gone wrong, so that Jesus was in tension with these ideas? Simply that man-imposed rules have a habit of becoming fixed and inflexible, of turning into dogmas and a cast-iron system that does not yield to change, and any infringement or failure meets with a harsh condemnation.

Jesus began His ministry with a new teaching (1:27). This was centered in the rule of God which brings joy and liberty, not restriction and judgment. His announcement was a gospel, the good news of "God's story" (Godspell), about God's love and His desire that we should live as His children in a family where we are trusted and accepted for what we are and what God can make us. This is the deep-down cleavage between Jesus and Jewish leaders.

On which side do I put myself? Jesus didn't say you shall know the rules and by them you shall be bound. But "you shall know the truth, and the truth shall make you free" (John 8:32).

Footnotes

1. William L. Lane, *Commentary*, p. 43.
2. J.M. Robinson, *The Problem of History in Mark*, p. 24.
3. See J.M. Robinson, *The Problem of History in Mark*, p. 46 and J. Kallas, *Jesus and the Power of Satan*.
4. U.W. Mauser, *Christ in the Wilderness*, p. 100.
5. R.P. Meye, *Jesus and the Twelve*, pp. 83, 99–110.
6. See Ralph P. Martin, *Mark: Evangelist and Theologian*, p. 121.
7. William L. Lane, *Commentary*, p. 86.

2
The Open Air Preacher

Mark 3:7—4:34

WHERE ARE WE GOING?

A writer several years ago commented that the two things about the earthly life of Jesus that were historically indisputable were (1) that He was a teacher of parables and (2) that He died on a Roman cross. If we had only non-Christian records, we should learn from Jewish and Roman sources that Jesus was known as a crucified teacher.

Already Mark has shown Him to be a man of action, taking the bold initiative and throwing down resounding challenges to the Jewish establishment. He is already a marked man whom the authorities are beginning to regard as too dangerous to have His freedom. For He makes great claims for Himself. He announces the arrival of God's rule on earth (1:14,15). He does what only God has the right to do (2:7). He takes up an attitude of indifference to the respected tradition of the scribes when that tradition runs counter to the demands of God's Kingdom (2:23–27, 3:1–6). And He teaches with a strange, compelling authority, displaying a charisma and power that invest His words with forcefulness and conviction (1:21,22).

So we turn to consider Jesus as Mark presents Him in His role as a teacher.

WHAT DOES IT SAY?

The first notice of Jesus' public teaching (1:21,22) is worth a second look. What impressed the worshipers at the synagogue in Capernaum was the directness and appeal of Jesus' teaching. Unlike their religious teachers who taught with "the authorities," He taught "with authority." They relied on what previous scholars had said, and built up an argument by quoting precedents and examples. He never quotes any source or book except the Old Testament and claims to understand it directly as His Father's word. Also, the scribes were known for their indecisive and hard-to-follow ways of teaching. He went right to the heart of an issue and gave plain answers to deep questions.

But Jesus was no dogmatic teacher, laying down the law with a firm, unyielding manner. He suited His message to the ability of the hearers, as 4:33 tells us. And He spoke in pictures, not in philosophical or legalistic tones as though He were unsure of a matter and seeking enlightenment from the hearers, or as if He were reading His teaching from a law book. These pictures we call parables.

But before we come to Mark's chapter of parables, we need to look at two matters in 3:7–31 that bear upon the theme of Jesus' teaching.

The Choosing of the Disciples/3:7–19

Up to this point in the public ministry, Jesus has conducted His mission either in the network of Galilean synagogues or in private conversation. There was nothing unusual in either method of teaching. In the synagogue service qualified teachers could be called upon to give a public address (as in Acts 13:15,16). Of course, Jesus was already getting a reputation for being a worker of mighty deeds of healing and He was already opposing the scribal rules concerning the Sabbath. He was immensely popular in Galilee, and this may well have prompted the decision to start an open-air ministry with a boat as His pulpit (see Mark 3:9,10).

But the door of the Jewish meeting-place is closing on Him. One of the chief reasons is not far to seek. Jesus was no "lone ranger," a kind of maverick preacher, moving across the Galilean towns and countryside as a solitary holy man. He had already begun to collect followers.

In His public ministry Jesus aimed at educating the special men He had chosen to be His disciples as much as He aimed at announcing to the general public what the Kingdom of God was all about. Mark records how Jesus called 12 men to be specially attached to Him (3:13–19). Their names are given. We have already met several of them before (1:16–20, 2:14); the rest are introduced for the first time.

We know Peter, and we will know him well before our reading of Mark's Gospel is through. The sons of Zebedee will reappear in the incident of Mark 10:35–40. The name "Boanerges" means in Hebrew "sons of tumult" (*benê regesh*) or "sons of wrath" (*benê rogez*). (See Luke 9:54 for one way in which they seemed to live up to this reputation for hotheadedness.) "Matthew" is the Levi of Mark 2:14. Bartholomew is sometimes identified with Nathaniel (John 1:45–51). "Simon the Canaanean" does not mean that he was a Canaanite, but a Zealot. He was, or had been, a member of the Zealots who stood for a holy war against Rome in the interests of regaining the political freedom of the Jews in Palestine. One carries an infamous title, "Judas Iscariot, who betrayed him" (3:19). He was probably a "man of Kerioth" in Judah. If so, he is the only one of the Twelve who was a southerner.[1] The others were Galileans.

The appointment of the Twelve is very significant. Only Mark tells us that Jesus delegated His messianic powers to them. Because of this authorization they are "sent out" (Greek *apostellein*, from which our word "apostle," meaning "missionary" or "one sent," is derived) to do just what their Master has been doing—preaching God's rule and driving out demons (1:39).

The Jewish leaders, we may guess, saw the intent of this move to select disciples. Jesus plans to commit His teaching to followers, and they in turn will transmit His message to a wider area. It is small wonder that the Jews are afraid of what the movement may become, especially when Jesus gives special teaching to the Twelve (4:34).

The Growing Opposition/3:20–35

The second factor affecting the theme of Jesus' teaching is the continuing activity of His enemies. They can't deny His mighty words and His indisputable success in healing the sick, expelling demons and overcoming evil. So they resort to innuendo and malicious gossip. They say that Jesus is in league with the devil, and that's why He can perform these cures.

The charge, "He is possessed by Beelzebul" (v. 22, *RSV*), is a powerful insult. "Beelzebul" is possibly a name for a demon, or it could be understood as an epithet or insult meaning "lord of dung" (Heb. *ba^cal zebûl*). In 2:28, Jesus had said, "The Son of Man is Lord even of the Sabbath." Here, the scribes were saying, "He is not lord of any Sabbath. The only thing he's lord of is the dung heap, and he's in cahoots with the devil and the demonic powers." It was a serious charge, and Jesus took it seriously.

His counter-argument is logical. In effect, He says, "If I am in league with Satan, as you say, why do I spend time in trying to destroy Satan's work by raiding his kingdom and setting the captives free?" Every confrontation with the evil powers has shown that Satan binds, but Jesus liberates. Since this is so, how can they, in all good sense, be partners together?

After the counter-argument comes a word picture of what Jesus is doing in relation to Satan's kingdom. Rather than being a partner with Satan, the Messiah will bind the strong man (Satan) and plunder his goods (3:27). Messiah is stronger-than-Satan, and He shows His authority over

Satan's forces by exorcising the demons. As the demonic influences are expelled, God's Kingdom is powerfully present (see Luke 11:20). Whenever God took over territory previously held by Satan, the demons had to cry out, "You are the Son of God," just as one day all demonic powers will admit that He is Lord (Phil. 2:9–11). Because Jesus knew that this tribute was being given involuntarily and under duress, he cautioned the demons not to spread it around (see Mark 3:11,12).

Then came His severest warning: "Whoever blasphemes against the Holy Spirit never has forgiveness, but is guilty of an eternal sin" (3:29, *RSV*).

Blasphemy[2] against the Holy Spirit is an attitude of resistance to the Holy Spirit, a rejection of God in human life and a perverse confusion of moral values and issues. Stephen pointed to an example of blasphemy when he said to those who would later kill him, "You always resist the Holy Spirit" (Acts 7:51, *RSV*).

In Jesus' teaching, it was blasphemy to attribute satanic powers to Him or to believe that He was none other than a false prophet inspired by the devil. To attribute His works of mercy, done in God's name to Satan, said Jesus, is to be morally perverse and spiritually blind. To say that He is the devil's Messiah is to cut oneself off from all understanding of who He is, and so to deny oneself access to God's forgiveness. This is the "unforgivable sin"—unforgivable because a person like this doesn't know what right and wrong are, and he is in no conscious need of being forgiven. He says, in effect, like Milton's Satan: "Evil, be thou my good."

So, there is still much opposition and a lot of confusion. Even His friends and family are persuaded that He is mentally unbalanced, and they try to restrain Him. His family is puzzled because they can't fit Him into the box they have constructed for Him. Verse 32 says that His mother came looking for Him. The Greek verb is "seeking," the same one used in reference to Peter when he approached the praying Jesus with the urgent plea, "Everyone is looking for you!" (1:37, *NIV*). It implies a hostile approach.[3]

Jesus responds, not unkindly, with the truth that natural kinship does not mean spiritual relationship. It is the latter —personal devotion and obedience to Christ—that saves. (See Luke 11:27,28 for someone who tried to flatter Jesus by a reference to His "wonderful mother." How did He respond?)

Teaching in Parables/4:1–34

With a new method of operation—open-air preaching (4:1)—there came a new style of public speaking—instruction by parables. Parables are vivid observations of nature and human nature. They speak of everyday, commonplace things, events, situations. Jesus tells a story, in the first place, to gain the hearer's attention, interest and sympathy. Then, His parables bid us take a further step. This is to consider the best in life as a hint of and then a stepping-stone to an awareness of what God is like. Thus, they set out a standard by which we can measure what we ought to be. "The parable," says T.W. Manson[4], "shows us what kind of God we must believe in and what kind of persons we must be." And, throughout all His parables, Jesus has His eye on false ideas about God's reign, and wrong-headed notions about the way that Kingdom comes to men and women. His parables are therefore not just pretty tales, to tickle our fancy or to entertain. They are counterattacks on current wrong ideas about God and His purposes. They are His "weapons of warfare," as J. Jeremias calls them[5], by whose power Satan's realm is invaded and his house robbed (see 3:27).

Let's take three parables which are consonant with Mark's message to his church.

1. The sower, the seed, and the soils (4:1–20) speak of the effectiveness of Jesus' own teaching. In a sense, it is a parable about the other parables. The sower sows good seed in every place. In some places the harvest is lost, but that is not the fault of the seed. The listeners in an agricultural society would have expected at least a bumper crop from any harvest. Jesus, however, expects much more than a bumper crop. He expects a bountiful harvest.

The lesson is clear. "Between Jesus' ministry apparently so modest, and the glorious coming of the kingdom of God, He establishes a cause-and-effect relation, comparable to that between the sowing and the harvest."[6] The tremendous harvest is a sure token that the new age of the Kingdom—what the Jews were looking for in the messianic age of bounty and blessedness, described in such Old Testament verses as Amos 9:13–15—is happening in Jesus' ministry. Jesus envisions here a great harvest in a worldwide church—a theme to be handled later in such verses as Mark 7:27; 11:17; 13:10 and 14:9.

In verse 11, "To you" refers to the disciples who have the privilege of hearing Jesus' application of the parables (v. 34). "For those outside" means the people who listen to a parable but who hear and understand nothing more than a good, interesting tale. If they were intent on "following through," they would face all types of opposition, such as Jesus gives in verses 14–20.

The Jewish people, in Mark's day, remained unresponsive, as Paul too found (Rom. 11:25). Paul's term for Israel's "hardness" (Greek *porosis*) is used at Mark 3:5 of the scribes' insensibility and opposition to Jesus. This blindness of Israel is part of the "mystery" that permits the Gentiles to hear the gospel and be included in the one church of God (Eph. 3:3–11).

Verses 13–20 give the report of Jesus' explanation of the preceding parable. We should notice how often—eight times—the "word" is mentioned. It stands for Jesus' proclamation of the Kingdom as a present reality in his person and mission (1:15). Also it represents the later apostolic ministry, declared by Paul to be the announcement of God's Kingdom into which believers in Jesus are called to enter (Col. 1:13) and whose experience is known in "righteousness and peace and joy in the Holy Spirit" (Rom. 14:17).

It is this message, given in both Jesus' earthly ministry and the apostles' preaching, that men and women either fail to grasp, or give only nominal assent to, or receive half-heartedly—or gladly and gratefully accept in full salvation.

27

The word is the same in each case. What differs is the "soil," or the person's life and the type of commitment he or she is willing to make.

That's why verses 23, 24 are a solemn warning. It all depends on *how* we hear what is said. The message is God's saving truth in Christ; what is called for is a serious, personal, life-changing response lest we miss the good things God's Word offers. Can a person miss these things? See Hebrews 4:2 for the answer: "The message which they heard did not benefit them, *because it did not meet with faith in the hearers*" (*RSV*, italics added).

Despite wastage, failure due to human unresponsiveness, and satanic countermeasures, however, there is a crop which will make the farmer's labor well worthwhile. It will be crowned with success at harvest, and that gives him encouragement to go on. So Jesus is not disheartened even if the results are meager for the moment. There will come a great harvest (see Rev. 14:17–19). Preachers in the early church, struggling to be faithful in time of persecution and falling away, would find consolation in this story of Jesus.

2. This little story of the seed growing secretly (4:26–29) is found only in Mark. The lesson is one of patience, which is the trademark of the farmer (see Jas. 5:7). He buries the seed in the earth and awaits the processes of germination, growth and fruitbearing to produce the harvest crop.

So God will take care of His Kingdom in His own way. There is no need for His people to be anxious, or to try to hasten its coming, as the nationalist Zealots were doing by taking up arms in a guerilla campaign against Rome. No more than a farmer wants to dig up the seed to see how it is faring do Christian preachers want to be overzealous to see "results." In both agriculture and pastoral ministry we may leave the issue with God whose "word" it is that is sown.

3. The third parable in this series is the story of the mustard seed (4:30–32) The mustard tree is usually taken to be the species *Brassica* or *Sinapis nigra*, or black mustard. It was cultivated in Palestine for both mustard and its oil produce. When it is grown in isolation, its height could

reach to 15 feet and its thick, main stem could easily support the weight of a flock of birds.[8]

This story teaches the inclusiveness of the rule of God, since "birds of the air" are symbols in the Old Testament (Ezek. 17:23; 31:6; Dan. 4:11,12,21) for the Gentiles. The Kingdom begins small but grows because it is God's Kingdom; and the tree, planted on Jewish soil, will soon spread out its branches to give shelter and hospitality to the "nations" beyond the borders of the Jewish people. This is another feature of Mark namely his interest in the wider outreach of Jesus' message. To the church in his day it would have obvious relevance.

Jesus, said the disciples on the Emmaus road as they were quizzed by the unknown stranger, was "mighty in deed and word" (Luke 24:19, *RSV*). We have seen something of His gracious words; in Mark 4:35–41 we have Him portrayed mighty in action. That can be our theme in the next chapter.

WHAT DOES IT MEAN TODAY?

Standing out in the verses of this section is Jesus' concern to get people to understand what His message was all about. His mighty deeds of healings could be misunderstood, and even explained away as the conjuring tricks of a fake therapist and magician. He had to repudiate and live down this allegation. He did so in several ways.

One was to try to keep His miracles of healing a secret. So He bids the demons not to advertise who He is (3:12). Then, He utters serious warnings about falsely attributing His power to evil forces, as though He were Satan's Messiah.

But His main line of work in clearing people's minds of wrong notions was His teaching. This teaching, in chapter 4, He gave by using lots of illustrations and examples drawn from real-life situations.

This section has its special appeal therefore to all who seek to teach God's Word in church, school and in small group and home Bible studies. Let's face up to some searching questions in light of our passage.

1. *The disciples will learn first, then teach others (3:14).*
Here is the sequence that cannot be broken. Only as we are called by Jesus and spend much time "with Him" shall we be able to go out in His name to preach with authority.

"You spoke as though you had just come out of the divine audience room," said a Presbyterian elder to the Scottish preacher, Alexander Whyte, as he came down from the Sunday morning pulpit. "Perhaps I did," he modestly affirmed. Only those who go "up" to their pulpit direct from Jesus' presence will come "down," having spoken with "authority."

2. Being in Christ's presence and hearing His matchless teaching must have been an inestimable privilege. Think of the chosen 12 disciples, later to become apostles. Then, imagine how fortunate the crowd must have been to hear Jesus speak in their hearing.

But is that enough? Remember that of 12 men, one turned out to be the traitor. He left the supper in the Upper Room where he had heard "wonderful words of life" (John 13—16), and went straight to betray his Lord. The crowd received Jesus' words like seed, but only one quarter of the seed fell on good ground. The rest was wasted because the soil was poor or stony or thorn-infested.

So there is nothing magical about "being with Jesus." What brings us His saving grace is our disposition of an eagerness to hear, a readiness to accept His teaching and to act upon it at whatever cost, and a willingness to give Him first place in our lives. (Read Matt. 7:24—27.)

3. Jesus is, above all else, concerned to get home to His hearers the truth of God's Kingdom and His rule in human lives. To proclaim that message is like the farmer sowing seed. But once it is sown, the farmer has to leave it in the earth, in hope that it will spring to life and in patience that it will grow in God's good time and way. Read James 5:7 whenever you get impatient with that Sunday School class of inattentive kids, or frustrated that so few church members have a desire to come out to midweek Bible studies, or when the deacon board is irritatingly slow and cautious to launch out with new programs.

30

God's Kingdom is *His* responsibility, and we can only do what we can, just as Paul plants, Apollos waters, but it is God who gives the growth (1 Cor. 3:6).

4. Then learn the big lesson from Jesus, the teacher, who never gave up patiently instructing people, seeking to clear their minds of wrong ideas and false hopes about God's Kingdom. He placed so much confidence in the spoken word, the personal influence of conversation, the vehicle of verbal communication.

The day of preaching is not over! It is still God's way to bring men and women, boys and girls to know Him (see 1 Cor. 1:21). While there are so many wrong, half-baked notions about God, Jesus, heaven, sin, and what makes a Christian, in folks' mind, it is our job to clear up the mess and let people *know the truth*, as God has made it known in Jesus Christ.

Remember: Kierkegaard, the Danish philosopher, said: "Wrongheaded ideas are like a cramp in the foot. The best cure is to stamp on them."

Footnotes

1. The author has discussed some problems associated with Judas in *New Bible Dictionary*, ed. J.D. Douglas, pp. 673–675.
2. "Blasphemy" is a difficult term to understand in the Bible. It is more than profanity or foul-mouthed talk. It means a godless attitude. See *New Bible Dictionary*, pp. 159, 160.
3. See Ralph P. Martin, *Mark: Evangelist and Theologian*, p. 168.
4. T.W. Manson, *The Beginning of the Gospel*, p. 41.
5. J. Jeremias, *The Parables of Jesus*, p. 19.
6. J. Dupont, quoted in *The Jerome Biblical Commentary*, ed. E.J. Mally, sec. 42.25.
7. On the matter of Mark's missionary interest in a world church, see Ralph P. Martin, *Mark: Evangelist and Theologian*, pp. 209–225.
8. See W.E. Shewell-Cooper in *Zondervan Pictorial Encyclopedia of the Bible*, vol. 4, pp. 324f.

3
Jesus Exorcist and Healer

Mark 4:35—5:43

WHERE ARE WE GOING?

God, said the psalmist (Ps. 65:7), "stills the roaring of the seas, and the tumult of the peoples." Mark's Gospel gathers together in an impressive cluster four stories of Jesus' power over nature and human nature, and man's last enemy, to show that Jesus does today what God did long ago.

WHAT DOES IT SAY?
Jesus, Master of the Wind and Sea/4:35–41

In Mark 4:35, Jesus Himself initiates the journey across the Sea of Galilee, with the words, " 'Let us cross over to the other side.' "[1] The lake is a pear-shaped inland sea, measuring 12 miles by 6 miles at its widest. Its coastline was inhabited in Jesus' day, and it provided a busy trade in fishing and the export of goods in several directions. Jesus summoned the first disciples here (1:16), as they engaged in fishing near Capernaum.

The sea of Galilee lies in a basin, and is subject to storms caused by the atmospheric pressure which, in turn, is created by the surrounding high mountains. Travelers tell how sudden storms frequently make this crossing an eventful occasion, and the winds sweeping across the lake are often encountered without warning. So, on this crossing, there was a great storm of wind, of gale force, which quickly had the small craft in danger (4:37).

Jesus was asleep in the stern—a human detail recorded only by Mark (4:38) as though to emphasize the true humanity of Jesus. He was no doubt worn out by the events of His public ministry. But there may be deeper meaning. In the Old Testament, the picture and promise of sleep in the midst of peril and disturbance is a token of a person's perfect trust in the sustaining and protecting care of God (see Ps. 4:8; Prov. 3:23,24; Job 11:18,19; Lev. 26:6). So it is Jesus' confidence in His Father's watchful care over the boat in which He rides that gives Him a poise and a serenity in the midst of the storm.

But the disciples rudely awaken Him, and speaking in words which have no specific parallel in the other Gospels, they take Him to task for His apparent negligence and disregard of their safety: "Teacher, are we to drown, for all you care?" (4:38 in *Moffatt's* vivid translation).

The disciples' petulant cry is full of criticism and annoyance. "The Son of God is subjected to the rudeness of men."[2] Mark wished to bring out the true humanity of both Jesus (who is exhausted and asleep) and the Twelve who speak their mind in harsh tones. It is a feature of Mark's Gospel that he grounds both Jesus and the persons he meets in real-life situations. Jesus is no character in a charade. Nor are the men Jesus called to follow Him like play-actors on a stage.

They had no need to arouse Him in this rude way. Jesus, as ever, is the Master of the situation. Mark's account is especially valuable, since it preserves the actual words Jesus used in calming the sea and quieting the raging winds. As though He were addressing a turbulent spirit which was agitating the watery deep, He commands, "Peace! Be still!"

(literally, "be muzzled," 4:39). The effect of these words is dramatic. The wind dies down and there is a great calm just as there had been a great storm earlier.

Mark wishes the reader to observe the difference Jesus makes. He is Lord of wind and waves, and He controls the dark forces of the deep which the Jews, who were no maritime people and until recently were a nation that boasted of no naval strength, feared as forbidding and unruly.

It is small wonder, then, that in the Old Testament one of the great attributes of God is that He controls the sea and subdues the chaos-monster that is associated with the deep ocean (see Ps. 89:9,10; 93:3,4; 106:8,9; Isa. 51:9,10). Best of all, in Psalm 107:23–30, we read of men who, like Jesus' disciples, cry to the Lord in their distress and are saved. It is only God who can pacify the unruly elements. Jesus acts in His own name to do just that.

After stilling the storm, Jesus takes the opportunity to question the disciples at the moment when they are still pondering the experience, and are most open to learning from it.

The best texts for what He said read: "Why are you so fearful? Do you *not yet* have faith?" (4:40). These are not questions asked for information, but to express surprise and consternation on Jesus' part that His men are still—even though they have seen His wonderful power—disbelieving.[3]

It is a tribute to Jesus' power over the chaotic elements that leads to the disciples' rhetorical question, "Who then is this, for even wind and sea"—two elements the Jews feared most—"obey him?" This is the big question raised by the story.

The answer comes back: This is none other than the Son of God, God's presence and power in human form. Jesus does what Yahweh does in stilling the sea. Not without reason the disciples are filled with reverence and awe (4:41).

In later years this account would be a comforting assurance to Mark's readers as they faced the demonic outrage of persecution, and as the little "ship of the church" (*navis*

34

ecclesiae, as one early church Father called it) is rocked in the storm and is almost swamped.

Jesus, the Exorcist/5:1–20

The cure of the Gerasene man who was sadly demented and demon-possessed is told with a wealth of personal and descriptive detail. Here we have in dramatic narrative the full account of what happened when Jesus encountered the irrational, psychotic forces of a split personality. But that is the modern way of putting it. The Gospel writers go deeper and attribute such derangement of personality to the possession of dark evil forces, called demons (see 1:32 where, as we earlier observed, sickness of body and demonic dominance of the human spirit are distinguished).

The Jewish scholars said that there were four features of madness in human behavior: (1) walking out-of-doors at night; (2) spending the night in a cemetery; (3) tearing one's clothes; and (4) destructive habits with gifts and one's person.[4] Most of these features are present in the man from Gerasa (*KJV*, Gadara), the modern Kersa or Koursi on the east bank of Lake Galilee.

When the man saw Jesus, he shouted, "What have I to do with you?" (5:7). This is an idiomatic expression, meaning "Why are you interfering with me?" Implied may be an off-handed threat, "Hands off me, mind your own business," as in Luke 8:28.

The man is full of fear that Jesus is bent on harming him, so he cries out for God to protect him from Jesus! He speaks in terms of what he knows of Jesus as "Son of the Most High God," a name that was "current coin" in Judaism outside of Palestine (see Acts 16:17 for a similar demonized person who greets Paul as a servant of "the Most High God").

The demons in the man respond to the challenge: "What is your name?" (Mark 5:9). A legion was a division of the Roman army, at least 6,000 men in strength. But the answer is probably to be understood as: "We demons are a great host," and we resemble one another as soldiers do when they are drawn up in squad formation.[5]

35

Jesus plays the role of the exorcist. This is a title for Jesus that, until recently, was locked away in the scholars' textbooks. Now, since the publication of William Blatty's novel and the film based on it, it is a word on many people's lips. The sad thing is that both the book and the film miss the really significant truth. Both are unhealthy exploitations of a serious theme, especially the film with its gruesome scenes and sordid detail which justify the newspaper review that it is a movie for "strong stomachs and weak minds."

The essential point, obviously missing from the modern attempt to portray exorcism, is Jesus' victory over demonic forces. In this story once more, He is in command of the scene, and knows exactly how to deal with the menacing approach of this poor, demented man. The courage of Jesus shines through, both in His call to the demon to leave this man (5:8) and His tactful conversation which centers in the identity of the name (5:9). The popular belief was that if the name of the demon could be known, its evil power was overcome.

Mark paints two cameos in unforgettable language. First, the state of the man in his manic depressive condition (5:2–6); second, the marvelous transformation that changed the demoniac in every way after the power of Jesus has been known and the man has been liberated (5: 15).

The question is often posed, "Why did Jesus order (or rather, permit) the destruction of the pigs?" (5:13).

Pigs were unclean animals for Jews in Palestine. But these pigs were the property of inhabitants who lived in Decapolis—a geographical description of some towns in northeastern Galilee—which had a predominantly Gentile population.[6] We can only reply that (1) the demons wanted to invade the swine according to the request of verse 12; and (2) in the scale of values, stated in another context in Luke 12:24, Jesus set a higher importance on preserving the life of the man whom the demons were destroying than on the fate of the pigs. There may be also a typological significance—intended to prove that the power which held the Gentiles captive was itself destroyed (cf. 1 Kings 18:40)

—as well as a demonstration to the man himself that his tormentors were taken care of in a way that could not be denied—by being drowned along with the animals.[7]

Mark's story is so true to life in telling that the people flocked out to see the miracle, and just as true to experience that the man, now a fully integrated person, should want to stay with Jesus (5:18). But Jesus has some better work for him to do—to tell others of God's power in his life (5:19), which he did (5:20).

The Gentile region of Decapolis needed to be evangelized. The geographical setting evidently explains why Jesus could command the news of the cure to be blazoned, while in Galilee He commanded silence as part of the "messianic secret" (see 5:43, a scene set in Jewish parts of the territory).

Jesus, Victor over Death and Disease/5:21–43

Jesus' power over disease and death is shown in two stories that Mark has run together. *The raising of Jairus' daughter is obviously the chief event.* Jairus is called one of the "rulers of the synagogue" (5:22). As such he was responsible for the conduct of the services and the management of the institution in the village where it served as school and courthouse on the weekdays.[8]

Jairus requested that Jesus come and lay hands on his daughter (5:23). The action of "laying hands" on the sick is not as common in the Old Testament and among the Jews as we might imagine. In fact, there are no cases where this action as a sign of healing and exorcism is performed earlier than the evidence of the Dead Sea Scrolls. (In a recently discovered document [the Genesis Apocryphon], Abraham lays his hands on Pharaoh's head, the demon is expelled, and he lives.) But the action was a feature of Jesus' ministry and later it became part of the apostles' work in Acts and the epistles (Jas. 5:13–16; note too the *KJV* verse in Mark 16:18).

In verse 24, we see Jesus going with Jairus to offer the touch of sympathy and to identify Himself with human needs.

37

One of the literary features of Mark's style is to sandwich one story between two layers of another story. The episode of the woman suffering from a hemorrhage is set within the framework of the Jairus story in this sandwich structure.

It is full of human interest (5:25–34). She interrupts Jesus as He is moving to the scene of what becomes a bereavement; her furtive approach and instantaneous cure, however, are not allowed to escape notice.

Jesus knew that it was a woman who had touched Him, and that she was different from the crowd who merely thronged around Him. "He looked about to see *her that had done this*" (5:30) is how the Greek reads. Then He draws public attention to her. "Who touched me?" is a question meant to pick her out from the crowd who merely rubbed shoulders with Jesus.

Her touching may have seemed more like superstition and wistful expectancy (in v. 28). But Jesus recognized it as genuine faith that brought results and recognition by Him (v. 34).

There is a distinction Mark perhaps intends us to see. It is one thing to be in Jesus' company—as a member of a Christian family or to be in a church service or to be identified with a group of believers. Yet the personal response we make as individuals who are drawn to Him out of a sense of deep need is the all-important thing. Thronging to Him is one thing; but touching Him in faith (see 5:34) matters far more.

So the woman is praised as she stands out in the crowd as a person who has personal and effectual faith, and she is sent back into life as a new person. She would no longer have to bear the stigma of a person ceremonially unclean (Lev. 15:25–30), and so an outcast from society.

Her bold approach in faith contrasts sharply with the unbelief of those who came to Jairus and told him, "Your daughter has died. Why worry the Teacher anymore?" Jesus' response to the report of the little girl's death is characteristic—He ignored it (5:36, *RSV*).

Literally, Jesus' words run: "Stop being afraid. Keep on believing." This was His way of reassuring Jairus that the

38

unfortunate delay in reaching the house was not something that He couldn't handle.

The commotion at Jairus' home when Jesus arrived (5: 38) was part of the death-lament ceremonies by which the deceased were mourned in Palestine. Professional wailing was practiced, along with choral chanting and handclapping.

Jesus understands the problem created by such a personal bereavement and family sorrow—to us so mysterious and forbidding, for there can be nothing more final and unrelenting than death. He assures the newly bereaved parents that the little one is "sleeping," which Mark intends the reader to understand as the "sleep of death" (as Paul does in 1 Thess. 4:13–15; 5:10).

Therefore, He dismisses the mourners as unnecessary. This provokes a jeer. The mourners can *see* that she is dead. The "jeering" may well have been part of the general attitude of unbelief, since to a person without faith in the living God, death is always final.

A similar verb is used of the Athenians who mocked Paul's message about the risen Lord (Acts 17:32). On that very site of Areopagus, the Greek god Apollo had declared in a well-known Greek play:

"Once a man is dead, there is no resurrection."

Jesus came to awaken the girl from that "sleep-in-death" and to restore her to new vigor and health. Using tender words exactly suited to the case, He speaks in Aramaic, His native language: "Little one, it's time to get up" (5:41), in tones as natural as a mother's morning call to a drowsy infant.

After she had arisen, Jesus ordered everyone to keep the incident secret (5:43). How could the miracle be kept a secret? We should probably follow T.W. Manson[9] in his understanding that two matters are involved here. The raising of the girl was plain for all to see. What Jesus wanted to remain under wraps was the way He had raised her, lest it should provoke a wave of popular superstition and lead to an unmanageable flow of requests for Him to raise the dead. This would distract from His chief mission, which was to proclaim God's rule in the now, and to issue a call to faith, not a superstitious belief in signs.

Yet He has compassion on Jairus, who gets his faith honored (v. 36). Jesus wants to help. At the same time, He is careful to avoid a popular uprising based on a false belief in Him as only a miracle-worker.

The lesson to the church of Mark's day and to us seems clear. Jesus is the Master of man's great enemy which, since the resurrection of Jesus on Easter morning, wears a different face. No longer is it menacing and to be feared (1 Cor. 15:54–57). Its power to harm the Christian is no greater than that of a sleep from which believers are awakened at the resurrection of the dead.

One short sleep past, We wake eternally.
And death shall be no more;
Death, thou shalt die.

John Donne

Three passages in this Gospel contain four dramatic stories. All center on Jesus in His powerful roles as exorcist, healer and Lord. All of them proclaim a central message to the church in every age. Man's great enemies—in his world and in himself—are powerless before the strong Son of God. Whether the foes we face are turbulent human nature in the grip of demonic elements, or the vexing, mind-bending issues of unruly and explosive natural forces that sweep across our planet earth, or the existential dread of facing the specter of death, the church's bold assertion of confidence is:

Thine be the glory, risen, conquering Son
Endless is the victory Thou o'er death hast won.

WHAT DOES IT MEAN TODAY?

In this section of Mark we are confronted with Jesus as a powerful actor in a moving drama. In quick succession story follows upon story in which He is on the move and engaged in dramatic episodes. Sometimes the circumstances are brought about by natural phenomena, such as the storm at sea. Jesus is in conflict with the uncanny world of the irrational, psychotic forces of the demonic. He is brought into touch with human suffering and need, and He faces a problem that remains man's greatest mystery, death.

These stories represent a cross-section of human experience that would be enough to throw any one of us off-balance, and give us a traumatic feeling of being threatened and overwhelmed. Yet Jesus takes it all in His stride. He never appears flustered, nor is He at a loss to know what to do. He doesn't appeal to others for advice, nor does He give the impression that He is groping for answers. He is master of every situation, and He is supremely confident in situations where lesser men and women would have gone to pieces. Let's look at the four cameo pictures to see some reinforcement of our confidence in Him as Lord of life and death.

1. He is asleep in the boat. Even when the storm breaks on the lake, He "keeps his cool." This causes great upset to the disciples, many of whom were fishermen and quite used to being caught in a boat on a turbulent sea.

He gets up and takes command of the situation, doing in His own name what God in the Old Testament does as Lord of the unruly natural elements.

For Jesus, however, it is just as true to say that He is master because of His real faith in God as to say that He acts as God does. His sleep in the presence of danger is a token of a perfect serenity that stems from His perfect trust in His Father.

Again, as in 1:12,13, He is the model believer, the ideal man, the living exponent of His own teaching and shining example of faith. (See Heb. 12:2: "Jesus, the Pioneer and Perfecter of our faith," *NIV.*)

We usually think of Jesus, the one whom we trust in, as the object of our faith. Let's see Him on the storm-tossed boat as the *model of faith in God.* Fear is driven out of His heart because faith is supreme (hence, the rebuke in Mark 4:40, where fear and faith are opposites). And because He trusts in God so completely, even in peril and when His life is threatened, He can summon us *to be like Him.*

2. The confrontation with the Gerasene demoniac is a

41

window through which we see the courage and strength of Jesus' character. Master of the scene and taking charge of the problem presented by this poor man and what he represented, Jesus firmly addressses the situation in the awareness that evil must yield to His presence, or rather, God's presence in Him.

The great change only comes about as the man is willing to face up to reality. Jesus' first approach was painful and the man feels threatened, crying, "Don't torment me" (5:7). Like a surgeon at work in an operating room, Jesus' intention was to wound in order to heal. His radical diagnosis pierces to the heart of the trouble, even if it causes momentary anguish. Yet His design is always for our final good and lasting healing. Consider the false prophets of Israel who "healed lightly" the troubles of the nation (Jer. 6:14), when Isaiah's more realistic diagnosis didn't please (Isa. 1:5,6). Or T.S. Eliot's moving description of the doctor's faithful mission:

The wounding surgeon plies the steel
That questions the distempered part;
Beneath the bleeding hands we feel
The sharp compassion of the healer's art,
Resolving the enigma of the fever chart.
                                        Four Quartets

Jesus' design is *to make men whole*, just as God wills that people should find fullness of life in fellowship with Him through Christ. So often we give the impression that God's purpose is meant to rob our lives of their happiness, that Christ is the world's master killjoy, and Christianity is like a prison. Just the opposite is true. He comes to set us free from our secret fears, inhibitions and complexes, and to remake us as *whole persons*.

Could there be a greater contrast than in 5:3–5 on the one side and in 5:15 on the other? It is the vivid contrast between what the man was and what he became—and that's the difference Jesus made. Which do we really want for ourselves, our family and our friends?

Don't worry unduly about the pigs—and so miss the real message. Deranged and distressed, this man was a menace

42

to society, a misfit in life, and a misery to himself. Now, once he has met Jesus, he gains self-respect, his manner is civilized and his influence will be considerable (5:16–20). Wasn't it worth the loss of the pigs?

One final note about Jesus and demons:

"There are two equal and opposite errors into which our race can fall about the devils. One is to disbelieve in their existence. The other is to believe and to feel an excessive and unhealthy interest in them."[10] We would do well to avoid both extremes.

3. In the story of the woman whose life was blighted and burdened by her illness and resultant "uncleanness" (making her a social outcast), we see the difference highlighted between the attitude of the crowd and of the one individual in the crowd who meant business. The crowd jostled and pushed Jesus as He moved down the village street. They were in a carnival mood, out for some excitement and curious to see a miracle in Jairus' home. The woman came close to Jesus for a different purpose. *She had a need*, and she drew near to Jesus as a last resort and a final hope. That's the way to come to Him:

What comfort can a Saviour bring
To those who never felt their woe?

She got from Jesus that day all she could ask for, and then some. Her bonus blessing was that she had a word personally addressed to her (5:34)—and that would be her passport into society once more. She expected to be cured and to slipback into the anonymity of the faceless crowd she had left. Instead, she was singled out and given a personalized miracle all to herself.

The crowd, eager to be spectators at the healing of Jairus' daughter, didn't even get a look-in. When the procession came to the house, they were all kept outside on the doorstep, cooling their heels. Only Jesus and the chosen three disciples went in with the father and mother (5:37,40).

Remember: Impersonal dealings with Christ always disappoint. Nothing is a substitute for a personal meeting, face-to-face and transforming. Second-hand religion never satisfies (see Acts 19:13–16). Only as each of us makes a direct, personal contact with Jesus can we know His life-changing power.

4. Death is still the number 1 issue in many people's minds. But it lies buried. A hundred years ago, sex was a taboo subject and hushed up in polite conversation, while the preparing for death was part of life's business. Now it's reversed. Sex is discussed at the least pretext, and death is pushed away from us and only discreetly introduced, if at all, as though we could avoid it if we tried!

The central thrust of the Christian message is to attack death's power to hurt us. The gospel doesn't deny death's reality and its solemn significance. It is an appointment we must all keep (Heb. 9:27). And it is related to sin, because sin pays its wages in death and death is "sin's sacrament" (said James Denney), the outward and visible sign of an inward and spiritual *dis*grace!

Yet Christ has conquered death, so the Bible affirms (2 Tim. 1:10). What that text means is to say that death's sting has been drawn, its power to harm us neutralized and its face changed. No longer an enemy to be feared, death is the entrance-gate to immortal life, if we believe that Jesus died and *lives again*, and because He lives, we too shall live in Him (John 14:19).

That's why death is a sleep from which the living Lord comes to arouse us and welcome us to His presence. So Paul can rejoice, "to die is gain" (Phil. 1:21).

Read again the scene in Jairus' home and catch the accents of Jesus' promise, "She is not dead but she is asleep." Match this with Paul's word that believers sleep in Jesus (1 Thess. 4:14,15)—not in unconsciousness, but in security. At the resurrection His commanding voice will awaken the departed dead as it did Lazarus (John 11:43).

Meanwhile, to die in Christ is to "fall asleep" as Stephen did (Acts 7:60).

Why be afraid of death? Let's renew our Christian confidence and assurance that to die, while it will be "an awfully big adventure," as Peter Pan said, is nothing more or less than to close our eyes on this life and open them to see Jesus!

44

Bishop Hannington, martyred for Christ in East Africa, told of his arrest that led to his eventual death: "I felt that they were coming upon me to murder me. But I sang 'Safe in the arms of Jesus,' and laughed at the agony of the situation."

People laughed at Jesus (5:40). Now, because of Jesus and His victory, Christians laugh at death (1 Cor. 15:54–57).

Footnotes

1. It is a good exercise to read Matthew's account (Matt. 8:23–27) of this story alongside Mark's. Notice the vividness and circumstantial detail in Mark. Does this suggest Peter's own retelling of the episode as an eyewitness?
2. William L. Lane, *Commentary*, p.176.
3. Faith is a key term in Mark, which we discuss in connection with 9:14–19. Also see Ralph P. Martin, *Mark: Evangelist and Theologian*, pp. 108–111. The background of the subduing of sea is found in G. von Rad, *Theology of Old Testament*, Vol. 1, pp. 150f.
4. See H. van der Loos, *The Miracles of Jesus*, pp. 386f.
5. See J. Jeremias, *Jesus' Promise to the Nations*, pp. 30–31.
6. See A. Alt, *Where Jesus Worked*.
7. Nevertheless, there are some residual problems here, as with the blasting of the fig tree in 11:12–14, chiefly to do with a miracle of destructive intent.
8. See Ralph P. Martin, *New Testament Foundations*, Vol. 1, pp. 80–83 for some details.
9. T.W. Manson, in *Studies in the Gospels*, ed. D.E. Nineham, p. 212.
10. C.S. Lewis.

Martyrdom
and
Misunderstanding
Mark 6:1-56

WHERE ARE WE GOING?

As an opening exercise in this study we look first at one of the noblest characters in the Bible's Hall of Fame, John the Baptist. Already we have learned from Mark's story that he came to be Jesus' herald and forerunner (1:2–8). Mark's Gospel gives him a special dignity as the preparer of the way who, in turn, was prepared for by the prophetic Scriptures.

In a combination of Old Testament verses drawn from Isaiah 40:3; Malachi 3:1 and Exodus 23:20, John's coming is foretold. When he came into the desert of Judea, he was greeted with an immediate response from the people (1:5); and yet he was careful not to claim too much for himself. He knew his place in history. It was to be a signpost pointing the way to the greater one to come (1:7,8).

Yet not everyone was pleased with John's message. So we must understand (reading between the lines) from the hint of his imprisonment and fate given in 1:14. Mark holds us in suspense as we wonder why John was so roughly treated, and what will happen to him. Now at 6:14–29 he will give us the answer to our questions in a sort of "flash-back."

WHAT DOES IT SAY?
John, the Martyr/6:14–29

The paragraph immediately preceding this account of Herod's brutal murder of John gives the reason for that story to be inserted here. Jesus has sent out the Twelve. They have enjoyed some success and gained popularity among the crowds in Galilee.

Herod now gets to hear of this religious movement which is linked with the name of Jesus, and wonders, quite naturally, who He may be. "Is He perhaps John the Baptist come back to life again?" he asks himself. (We accept the reading in verse 14, "he, Herod, was saying," not "men were saying." It has strong textual support.)

Mark had a reason for bringing out the comparison between Jesus and John. "The identification of Jesus with John, through whom the ancient gift of prophecy had been affirmed after so long a silence, appears to interpret Jesus as the promised eschatological Prophet whose word would herald the last days."[1] This leads Mark to report in some vivid detail John's martyrdom.

The man whom John annoyed most of all was Herod Antipas called a king. He succeeded to his father's control of Galilee on the death of Herod the Great in 4 B.C. Herod "the king"—a courtesy title granted by the Romans—was married to a daughter of the Nabatean king, Aretas, but he had also made an immoral union with his niece and sister-in-law, Herodias. He had met her in Rome when she was the wife of his half-brother Herod Philip, and had persuaded her to marry him after he abandoned the Nabatean princess. This is the background to Mark 6:17–20.

John's outspokenness at the way Herod had played around in high society was full of courage. He boldly denounced the immoral practices of both parties of "swingers."

47

Herod was a strange mixture of a man displaying a combination of secret fear and outrageous behavior that he had no doubt inherited from his father. Hence, he is typically in character in verse 20, which says that he couldn't make up his mind about John. He both respected and hated him.

Herodias, however, had no scruples at all. Her attitude was strictly personal and selfish, and she was determined to safeguard her own position as Herod's spouse. She knew, therefore, that "the only place where her marriage certificate could safely be written was on the back of the death warrant of John."[2]

This awareness explains her ploy, involving her daughter at Herod's birthday celebration (6:21–28). In a swift action Herod was caught off-guard in a compromising situation. The daughter's request for John's death is accepted to save his face, and a sad train of events follows. A rash promise from this half-drunk king was picked up by an eager request from a woman with a guilty conscience. This led to the willing cooperation of a girl who blindly obeyed her mother, and in turn there followed a hurried execution.

The Jewish historian Josephus[3] has a parallel story of John's death, which attributes Herod's hostility to political motives, as though John were seen as a threat to the security of the state. Mark's version has more personal motives involved, yet the two reports are not inconsistent, though the evangelist does make much of Herodias' jealousy.

A.E.J. Rawlinson comments:

> Both (accounts) are no doubt *bona fide* and independent: It is a mistake to try to harmonize the two. Josephus' version will give the facts as they presented themselves to a historian who wrote sixty years later, and who was concerned to trace the political causes of a war (the Jewish war of independence, A.D. 66–70). The story in Mark will be an account, written with a certain amount of literary freedom, of what was being darkly whispered in the bazaars or marketplaces of Palestine at the time."[4]

So John, man of God, herald of Jesus, preacher of righteousness, is ushered into God's presence. Surely all "trumpets sounded for him on the other side," as John Bunyan so fittingly described the death of another hero of the Christian faith.

John's disciples lay their master's body to rest, and they went off to tell Jesus (Matt. 14:12). Jesus' actions at the news are full of historical interest, for the immediate sequel is the Feeding of the Crowd. But this is only one item in a chapter of sad misunderstandings, and we should backtrack to the earlier verses.

Rejection at Nazareth/6:1–6

"He went away from there and came to [his native place]" (Mark 6:1, *RSV*), the little Galilean village of Nazareth. Jesus has already picked up something of a reputation. His mighty works are becoming well known, so it is not surprising that when He comes home to His native Nazareth, the unsolicited tribute is that He is both a teacher of great wisdom and a powerful healer (6:2). "What mighty works are wrought by his hands!" (*RSV*) they say, as they pay a tribute to Him that cannot be denied.

The people can't disprove His effectiveness. But they are puzzled about Him. After all, He is only the village carpenter turned preacher (6:3). The reference to Jesus as "the carpenter" is not paralleled in the other Gospels, which say simply that He was "the carpenter's son," i.e., Joseph's son, in the manner of human descent. The Markan text is the most realistic, since it clearly makes Jesus a manual worker, either in wood or iron.

Church Fathers like Origen were upset by this, and tried to deny that Jesus was an artisan. But Mark's witness, found in the best manuscripts, stands.

At least one reason for the cool rejection Jesus received in His hometown lies just here. The people were scandalized that a workingman should do works of power that claimed that God's Kingdom had come in His person and presence. That claim was more than they could take. So they refused Him.

49

And if Luke 4:16–30 refers to the same incident, then we see how they totally rejected Him, as men and women do today because He did not come with a heraldry of pomp and power and to be a popular leader or dictator-figure. Rather, He seemed to be just an "ordinary" prophet-preacher whose compelling authority lay in His self-giving service and His special relationship to God as His Son (see Mark 10:45). There was no halo around His head, and His feet touched the rough Palestinian soil at every point. This is the emphasis given by Mark's Gospel throughout its story.

A second reason for the Nazareth people to be disturbed was apparently the rumor that Jesus was illegitimate. There's nothing special about His family. This is the meaning of "Son of Mary." "No man in the East, whether his father were living or not, would be known familiarly by reference to his mother."[5] Calling Jesus in this way was a calculated insult.[6]

To call a man the son of his mother was to insult him by suggesting that he was born to an unmarried mother. Not surprisingly, then, they were deeply shocked at Him. In fact, says Mark, it was a stumbling block (the same Greek word as in 1 Cor. 1:23) on the road to faith.

The Nazareth townsfolk stumbled over His lowly origin and they never came to believe Him. In such a hostile atmosphere His power to perform "mighty deeds" (Greek *dynameis*, a key tèrm in this Gospel for deeds of power that herald the Kingdom's presence and reality in human experience) was restricted. Their unbelief set a brake on His ministry of healing and blocked the outflow of His power. His cures at Nazareth on "a few sick people" (6:5) were due to His compassion. But they carried no messianic meaning.[7]

So, "He *was astounded* at their unbelief." This is a strong verb, used only in this verse by Mark to describe Jesus' bitter disappointment. We are in touch here with the fully human Jesus whose feet were firmly planted on solid earth even to the point of His inability to do His works (v. 5). He didn't walk with His feet two inches off the ground, but He shared all our disappointments, frustrations and setbacks, as a true man among men and women. (Read Heb. 2:9–18 for one of the clearest statements in the New Testament of the full humanity of the Lord Jesus. It is an antidote to the first heresy in the Church—docetism, which was a denial of His complete humanness and a belief that He only "seemed" to be human, like a piece of playacting and a charade.)

Jesus and the Twelve/6:7–13,30–32

Right from the start of His public ministry, Jesus was intending to share that work with others. He was no solo performer who acted on the stage of history as a virtuoso, possessed with a sense of His own self-importance and exhibiting ostensible bravura. He has called 12 men to be His companions (3:13,14). Now He will give them a chance to do His works as He sends them out in His name (6:7,8) The men are to travel light and to accept the hospitality the village inhabitants offer them.

Not everyone will show that friendly spirit, and where there is indifference or hostility, the disciples are to quit the scene, because opposition to Jesus' message through their preaching says more about those who refuse it than about the validity of the message or the character of Jesus' representatives (6:10,11).

The action of the disciples when they're rejected is to leave the inhospitable city in a hurry and wipe off the dust from their feet "for a testimony against them" (6:11), i.e., as an act of incrimination and judgment, as in 13:9.[8] Pious Jews shook off the dust of the roads on entering the holy places of Temple and synagogue, so there may be a play on the words here. The apostles are to wipe their feet clean before continuing their mission, which is their holy business. The rejecting cities will be "unclean," and placed under self-inflicted condemnation.[9]

When the men came back, they reported on the great success of their mission (6:30). The work was exacting and stressful, so much so that Jesus saw the need to get them away on their own for "rest and recreation" (6:31). The

51

physical strain had taken its toll, but there may be a deeper reason for coming away to a lonely place. Jesus sensed that the disciples were agog with excitement, and that, flushed with the taste of success in their ministry of exorcism and teaching, they were easy prey to the idea that they could themselves promote a popular uprising of the Galilean masses.

Here we touch upon a very real issue in the unfolding Gospel narrative; *Jesus was just as much embarrassed by His friends as He was threatened by His enemies and misunderstood by the crowds.* The proof of this thesis—if a person has friends like these, who needs enemies?—will be seen in the next-in-sequence story of the feeding of the 5,000.

The Feeding of the Crowd/6:34–46

If we needed further proof that Jesus came to disappoint human hopes as well as to fulfill them, we should look no further than this story. The current expectation among the Jews was for a leader who would come to put an end to grinding poverty in a society that was squeezed by taxation, and expel the hated Roman overlords who levied the taxes and defiled the land of Israel with their armies.

The temptations in the desert (told in Matt. 4:1–11 and Luke 4:1–13) pinpoint the issues. Would Jesus turn stones into bread and create a new utopia of plenty? Would He stun people into belief with a breathtaking feat? Would He bring in God's Kingdom by using Satan's methods of military conquest? He rejected every idea of a quick victory. In reply to the devil's plan and proposals, He said firmly: There is no easy way to save the world.

Let us remember that these temptations came to Him throughout His ministry. Several points in the narrative of verses 34–46 indicate that this could have been the setting for a severe temptation and a major crisis in His ministry.[10]

The "many," in verses 31,33, who keep coming and going, appear to be laying plans for a messianic uprising. This is confirmed by their hurrying together to meet Jesus in verse 33, which suggests a widespread, premeditated and united movement.

Now, faced with a hungry multitude, Jesus shows His compassion and concern (6:34). They are like sheep with no shepherd. This suggests a congregation without a pastor to guide them; but strictly the metaphor refers to a leaderless mob like an army without a general (Num. 27:17; 1 Kings 22:17).

So the teaching of Jesus referred to in verse 34 could be His attempt to damp down the popular enthusiasm for revolt, raised to a fever pitch, and to act as a counterpoint to the current expectations.

The people are a danger to themselves and to everyone else if they get out of hand and start a violent anti-Roman demonstration, especially in Galilee where the nationalistic Zealots first raised the standard of revolt in the time of Judas the Galilean in A.D. 6. (Read Acts 5:37.)

So Jesus faced a double challenge. He wanted to help the crowd who had followed Him until they were weary and famished. Yet He sensed the danger. To give the impression that He was a second Moses, providing free manna in the desert—as the Messiah was expected to do especially at Passover time (a time-notice seen in Mark 6:39, when the grass was green in the springtime), according to the Jewish writings—would be to inflame their passions and give a wrong idea of what He claimed to be and what He had come to do.

Incidentally, the seating arrangements in verse 40 are not a catering convenience but a drawing up of people in a military formation "in rows by hundreds and by fifties," like the Israelite tribes in Exodus 18:25; Deuteronomy 1:15; and the sectarian forces at Qumran in the Dead Sea Scrolls (1 QM 4:2; 6:11: "Write [on the standard] the name of the chief of the Hundred and the names of the leaders of its Fifties").

We may have to read between Mark's lines and use some imagination, but the matter is made crystal clear in John 6:1–14. In John the feeding of the crowd leads to the abortive action of 6:15. They wanted to make Him king, but He fled from their enthusiasm, for He would not be a king on a "bread basis."[11]

The "I AM" in the Storm/6:47–56

Hence the sequel to the story as we come back to Mark 6:45,46. He dismissed the crowd; He ushered His disciples, somewhat against their will, into a boat because it is likely that they shared the crowd's aspirations and perhaps egged them on to bring out a crown for Jesus. Then He retired for prayer. Alone on the hillside He would resolve afresh that the road to success runs by way of the cross. Any other road is a snare and a false trail.

Later, Jesus came to the disciples, "walking on the sea" (6:49). In the Old Testament this is a manifestation of the divine presence.[12]

As He drew close to them, they were struck with great fear. When they saw Him, they cried out in terror. Jesus reassured them with some tender words, "Courage! It is I. Don't be afraid" (v. 50). It is not surprising that Jesus' identification of Himself should be couched in the language of the divine epiphany of the I AM presence (Exod. 3:14; 6:6; Isa. 48:12, picked up in John 8:24).

Mark's comment at the close of the stilling of the storm is highly significant. The disciples were at a loss to understand just who Jesus was, because "they did not understand about the loaves, but they had insensible, obtuse minds" (v. 52).

What was it about Jesus that puzzled them? The answer is that they were still looking at Him as a religious opportunist, ready at a moment's notice to gain a popular following and lead the people in a crusade of political liberation. What they failed to grasp was that in this person, Jesus of Nazareth, God Himself, the I AM presence of the Old Testament, was coming close to men, to deliver them from satanic bondage and demonic evil; and their real enemy was inside their lives.

So they failed to see this—until the cross brought down in ruins their nationalistic hopes and selfish, personal ambitions. Yet unlikely folk—like the sick in the Galilean countryside (6:53–56)—glimpsed the saving truth, even if there was a lot of superstition and false faith still mixed up with a genuine appreciation of Jesus' mission in the world.

54

WHAT DOES IT MEAN TODAY?

This long and important chapter in Jesus' life story raises some challenges for us to face in our life and service.

1. Have we really settled the matter in our attitudes to the gospel ministry that there is an "offense of the cross" (Gal. 5:11) that cannot be avoided, and that Jesus creates hostility and opposition when He lays His claims upon us? That's why His call was "Blessed is he who takes no offense at me" (Matt. 11:6, *RSV*).

While we do well to accentuate the wonderful offer of the good news and strive to make the invitation of Christ as attractive as possible to our generation, there is always the other side. Jesus Christ disappoints men's hopes as well as fulfills them.

Let's beware of any easygoing presentation of the message that soft-pedals the serious claims He makes, forgets the shadow-side of those demands of Christ, and that too quickly removes the stumbling block that Jesus puts in the way. Read again what happened at Nazareth (6:1–6). There was no eager welcome, but a cool rejection, and Jesus got the cold-shoulder treatment in His native place. They were disappointed in Him, and He was profoundly shocked at their attitude.

2. John the Baptist (6:17–29) and Peter (Acts 12:1–17) both experienced the hardship of prison, and both were under sentence of death. John paid the price in a martyr's death; Peter got release by God's intervention and the church's praying. Why should one go free, and the other face the prospect of death, where doubts and fears arise (see Matt. 11:2–6)?

Shall we turn this thought into prayer for imprisoned Christian leaders today for whom there is no deliverance?

3. Read 6:35,36. The crowd was hungry and tired. When folk are in that condition and the promise of a quick solution to their economic and social needs is dangled before them, they'll rise to the bait.

That's why Jesus faced in this desert scene, in the presence of the 5,000, the same temptation He confronted in another desert in the presence of Satan (Matt. 4:1–4).

The devil insinuated this idea to Him at that time: "Why not take the matter into your own hands, work your own miracles, and then announce to a people, struggling on the borderline of poverty and economic hardship, that the new age of God's plenty has come? Feed the crowds, and win their immediate allegiance with your slogan, 'No More Hunger.' You'll have the world at your feet overnight, and they'll hail you as the great Benefactor, the architect of a utopia of peace and plenty for all, and for free."

Jesus saw the danger. It was the snare of the shortcut. It offered an easy road to popularity and staked its claim on the undeniable truth that whatever panders to human appetites—physical, emotional, aesthetic, volitional—is bound to be applauded. But for Jesus this was not the way ahead.

Men need bread. Jesus gladly fed the multitude, and He acknowledged this human need. But He knew that there is no guarantee that any person who comes for the loaves and fish wants to hear the divine Word. So He could not accept the crown on the basis of His compassion as social benefactor and provider of free meals. The only crown that wins our true allegiance is the crown of thorns.

Footnotes

1. William L. Lane, *Commentary*, p. 212.

2. T.W. Manson, *The Servant Messiah*, p. 40.

3. *Antiquities* XVIII, V, 1–2.

4. A.E.J. Rawlinson, *Commentary*, p. 82.

5. E.F.F. Bishop.

6. R.H. Lightfoot, *History and Interpretation in the Gospels*, pp. 187f.

7. See for a discussion: Ralph P. Martin, *Mark: Evangelist and Theologian*, pp. 122–24, 169–71.

8. See Ralph P. Martin, *Mark: Evangelist and Theologian*, p. 223.

9. See T.W. Manson, *The Sayings of Jesus*, p. 76, and Acts 13:51.

10. Further details are given in a suggestive essay by H. Montefiore, "Revolt in the Desert? Mark vi. 30ff." *New Testament Studies*, 8, 1961, pp. 135–41.

11. G. Campbell Morgan.

12. See Psalm 77:19; Job 38:16; Isaiah 43:16, especially when it is set in a night vision when God draws near (Job 4:13–16; 9:8,11).

5
What Went Wrong?

Mark 7:1—8:26

WHERE ARE WE GOING?

So far, in our reading of the Gospel of Mark, we have seen that Jesus has few real friends; there is an excitable crowd who tag along behind Him to have their curiosity satisfied, and there are on the scene several groups of enemies. Indeed, those who claimed to be His friends, the chosen disciples, are full of wrong ideas and what little they understand of Jesus is apt to get lost amid the false hopes they entertain. They, like the crowd, think of their Master as a wonder-worker and a national leader who needed, above all else, a good public relations agency to promote His cause in Galilee. They can't believe how it was that, at the feeding of the 5,000, He let slip the marvelous opportunity to win the crowd.

The same failure to grasp what Jesus was doing in His public mission is seen in some modern biographies and highlighted in a recent popular version of the Jesus-story. Judas Iscariot sings, in the Webber-Rice rock opera, *Jesus Christ Superstar:*

Every time I look at you I don't understand,
Why you let the things you did get so out of hand.
You'd have managed better,
If you'd had it planned.

So we read of the Twelve in 6:52: "Their hearts were hardened," and so many readers of the Gospel story secretly wonder whether Jesus missed His chances and why He never became "Superstar." They need, therefore, to look closely at our passages today, as we ask: *What went wrong?* We shall zero in on three sections in particular.

WHAT DOES IT SAY?
Jesus Faced Religious Fanatics/7:1–23

When we last met the Pharisees, the religious leaders of Jesus' day, they were plotting His downfall (3:6). Now we learn why they were deeply disappointed in Him and how they came to turn against Him. It is just as true that Jesus must have found them to be a discouragement. They, of all people, should have recognized His claims and responded to His call. Instead, they criticized Him (7:5) and He found fault with them (7:9). The gulf between them was vast, and it grew wider as His ministry progressed.

The issue came to a head over two matters that the Pharisees held dear. Indeed, pharisaic religion could be summed up by those two items: (1) ceremonial purity (7:1–4)[1] and (2) the sacredness of vows (7:10–13). Together, with other concerns that made the Pharisees a group devoted to the serious pursuit of Jewish religion, these two items were part of "the tradition of the elders" (7:3). This body of authoritative rules and regulations had grown up alongside the Mosaic law and was like an explanatory commentary. It showed how the biblical law given in Moses' time was to be applied to real-life situations in the now.

For instance, the law required a holy people (Lev. 19:2;

58

Deut. 14:2). But what's holiness, and how can a person be "holy" in everyday living? The answer was given in the way Jews were to be particular over the washings of hands and the scouring of pots and pans.

Let us take a closer look at what the Jews meant by ceremonial purity. Verse 3 says, "They wash their hands." Then follows the Greek word *pygmé*, which is not translated in *RSV*. It may mean "as far as the wrist" or "with cupped hands" more than "oft," "repeatedly" (as *KJV* renders). But no one knows the precise meaning for certain. What is clear is that the Jews practiced a thorough cleansing, as they tried to rid themselves, not of germs but of ritual defilement, before a meal.

A person could get "defiled" in the eyes of the law by close contact with non-Jewish foreigners whose shadow falling across kitchen utensils and food could make them "unclean." All those prescriptions were carefully spelled out (as vv. 3,4 say) and this ritual to ensure that food was always kosher, that is, ceremonially fit to be eaten, was put alongside the law in authority.

Effectively quoting Isaiah's critique of the false religionists of his day (Isa. 29:13), Jesus found fault with this devotion to the "tradition of the elders." He was as committed to God's Word as any of the Pharisees. Precisely for that reason, He saw the danger when people elevate their manmade ideas to the level of Scripture and concentrate on the outward instead of the inward. This leads to superficial religion which is only for show, and forgets the great principle of 1 Samuel 16:7: "Man looks on the outward appearance; but the Lord looks on the heart" (*RSV*). Jesus had a stern word of rebuke (Mark 7:9) for this interest only in the facade and the external trappings of religion.

Secondly, the Pharisees made much of vows, especially where money or a property could be "dedicated" (the Aramaic work *korban*, 7:11)[2] to God or the Temple treasury. Even if the owner retained it, as he was entitled to, it could not be used for charitable purposes or put back in circulation even if his father or mother needed it. Korban was, as we say, a "cop-out," since the possessions were safe in a man's name and could not be touched. Thus a mean person could evade the most pressing of all obligations—care for parents in old age.

Jesus blasted this device as evil, and recalled the first responsibility we all have in family life, to "honor our parents" and care for them. No so-called religious duty can take precedence over that, or give us an escape clause to evade our fundamental duty of love.

Mark's editorial note in verse 19—"Thus he declared all foods clean"—draws attention to the great significance of what Jesus had just said and taught. In a word, it is not what we eat that matters, but what we say, as our words indicate our character (Matt. 12:35–37). This revolutionary teaching implied the canceling of all the elaborate food and dietary laws contained in Leviticus 11 and Deuteronomy 14, as interpreted by the rabbis.

The question of the permanence or otherwise of this side of the law of Moses was a live issue in the early Church (as we can see from Galatians 2:11–17; Romans 14:14–23; Colossians 2:20–22; Hebrews 13:9,10), and formed the main item on the agenda of the Jerusalem Council in A.D. 49 (Acts 15:19–21). Paul's battle with the Judaizers centered partly on this matter, and we can read his mind on questions of food in 1 Corinthians 8:4–13; 10:23–33; 1 Timothy 4:3–5.[3]

The really essential parts of faith can be summed up in a single phrase: What a man is in his inner life really counts (vv. 14–23). The worst defilement is a dirty mind; the best cleansing is that which is applied to the springs of the inner life, which God sees.

Jesus Would Not Restrict God's Love/7:24–37

He put into practice what He proclaimed. He had said there was no contamination except with evil thoughts, motives, and actions. So we find Him reaching out to a woman of the Gentile nation of Phoenicia on the Mediterranean coast, a person whom the Palestinian rabbis regarded as religiously unclean. She comes to Jesus with the problem of her sick child and asks for help.

60

Jesus tests her real desire by first refusing on the grounds that His mission was to the Jews, God's children (v. 27). "Let the children [Jews] *first* be satisfied." The italic word is not in Matthew's account (Matt. 15:26), and it would appear that Mark's inclusion of it gives priority to the interest of Jesus in reaching out to Jews. But "first" leads on to the "second," and that holds out hope for the non-Jews, represented in the Syrophoenician woman.

She reminds Him that in a house, at mealtime, at the moment when all attention is given to the children, the dogs are permitted to eat whatever food falls as scraps on the floor. In other words, she sees that Jesus' coming into the world is much bigger than a ministry to Jews. She was a member of a race whom the Jews called "Gentile dogs" and yet she believed she had some share in Him. She claims this as a privilege. And she is rewarded. Jesus praises her quick-witted repartee—and faith (v. 29).

Mark's readers would get the message. The gospel began in Galilee, but it is for those in Rome and throughout the world no less, and for all men and women everywhere. The same principle was built into Paul's missionary strategy (Rom. 1:16).[4]

Small wonder the Jewish leaders detested Jesus' work. It meant the end of all exclusive religious privileges and rights, and this teaching on the universal concern of God for all races would open the Kingdom of heaven to all believers, both Gentiles and Jews alike, on the basis of need, not merit. (Read Mark 2:17).

The same lesson shines out in the next paragraph, describing the man who had a speech defect caused by his chronic, congenital deafness (7:31–37). The setting is still on land that the Jews abhorred as pagan. "Tyre and Sidon" would conjure up bitter memories of Queen Jezebel, who led her husband King Ahab off the straight and narrow path long ago (1 Kings 18:17—21:29). True, the man resided in Decapolis, the semi-pagan part of Galilee, but that was regarded as no better than pagan territory.

Jesus stretched out a healing hand to him, even though he was a lost case, from the strict Jewish standpoint. Two points to notice, just under the surface. The man's condition (in v. 32) is described by a rare word meaning "stammerer," found only here and in Isaiah 35:6 where in the messianic age of blessedness the "tongue of the *dumb* shall sing."

The Messiah was expected both to open blind eyes and release dumb lips, according to Isaiah 29:18; 32:3f.; 42:7; 61:1; Ezekiel 24:27. Jesus applied healing power to this man's need, with the result that "he spoke plainly" (v. 35). He joined the others in the praise of God, who is at work in Jesus Christ, who does what God does.

The tribute vocalized in verse 37, "He has done all things well," is a distinct echo of Genesis 1:31, where God is well pleased with His creation. Jesus is thereby praised for doing God's work in healing even semi-pagan sick and needy folks, in a Gentile environment. This incident is another telltale sign that God and Jesus are brought together in Mark's Gospel.

Jesus Refused to Supply His Credentials/8:1–13

The prologue to the debate in 8:11–13 is a feeding of the crowd that is parallel to the earlier feeding (6:35–44). But there are differences.[5] Most noticeably the number is 4,000, not 5,000, and there are seven, not five loaves available. More significantly for its interpretation, the setting is non-Jewish. This suggested to Augustine, back in the fifth century, that the second story was designed to portray Jesus as the bread of life to the Gentiles.

With such a Gentile locale as the Decapolis region (in 7:31; 8:10), and the stress given to the hunger of the masses in verses 1–4, it seems clear that Mark wants to emphasize the outreach of Jesus to those who had little understanding of the messianic hope of Israel. "Some of them have come a long way" (v. 3, *RSV*)—from a distance—will then say the same as Paul's words in Ephesians 2:13, that the Gentiles, "who once were far off [the same Greek word underlies both verses] have been brought near in the blood of Christ" (*RSV*).

Verses 11–13 are a short paragraph, but they are full of

interest in the ongoing struggle between Jesus and His enemies. The Pharisees come to start an argument.[6] The issue turns on whether He is really a prophet come from God. If He has indeed come from God, would He kindly oblige the Pharisees in a way that Moses had laid down: Would He give them a sign from heaven—that is, a God-given phenomenon that would accredit Jesus, like a hand-writing in the sky?

Jesus refused point-blank. Not because He *couldn't* do what they were demanding, but because He *wouldn't*—at least not in the way they were expecting, and not for the reason they gave.

They were insincere and wanted only to trip Him up. Their request was a temptation (8:11). It was the old story of the devil's insinuation at the outset of Jesus' ministry (Matt. 4:1–11: Luke 4:1–13), inviting Him to jump down from the Temple parapet and float gently to a safe landing in the Temple area, upborne by the arms of the angels of God.

Jesus again disappointed these men, for a reason that is not far to seek. No amount of "proof" or demonstration will convince a person who has already made up his mind to disbelieve and who is evilly disposed against the truth. Only God can change his outlook. "Signs" will do no good. A person who is bent on disbelieving will always try to explain away the marvelous sign and say that it is done by magic or clever conjuring tricks or that he has heard and seen other people do the same thing (as in Matt. 12:27; Luke 11:19).

This is exactly what Paul found in 1 Corinthians 1:18–30. The Jews there and here in Galilee were looking for "signs" (1 Cor. 1:22) to convince them. But, said Paul, we offer only Christ on His cross (1:23) and we trust God to reveal His wisdom and power in a message that is apparent fool-ishness to the "man of the world," the natural man of 1 Corinthians 2:14.

So Jesus came into collision with leaders of the Jewish church and incidentally with the hopes cherished by the disciples, according to 8:14–21. They were still woefully ignorant and blind when it came to figuring out who their master really was. They seemed to be attracted to what Jesus criticized as the leaven (or false teaching) of the Pharisees, and He had to give them a stern warning.

He recalled the two feeding "signs" by which He had shown Himself to be the true Messiah of Israel and the provider of spiritual food for the Gentiles. He was no earthly king, offering simply temporal provision.

The key to Jesus' attitude lies in His questions about the loaves used to feed the crowds, and the broken pieces picked up by the basketful. That is symbolic, and it looks forward to the Upper Room meal when Jesus will take the bread and break it as a token of His body (14:22) to be given over to death for them and the Gentiles ("the many" of 10:45) on the cross. That is the secret mission He has come to fulfill, and they are too dim-witted to see it, because their minds are still obsessed with worldly ideas and they are wrangling over petty concerns (8:16).

But the real enemies are the Jewish religious leaders, the theologians of the day. They clung to their religious code and traditions, whereas He went to the heart of true religion, which is the religion of the heart. They were jealous of their ancestral privileges which excluded all non-Jews; He recognized human need and faith across national frontiers and ethnic boundaries. They wanted His fingerprints on a certificate of orthodoxy, but He turned away to set His face to go to Calvary. And the lonely cross on the hill is the only sign still to our world that *Jesus is God's message of love to all men.*

Mark's artistry is never more clearly seen than in what follows. The crowds misunderstand Jesus' purpose, and the chosen Twelve are led astray by false notions and need to be warned off the "leaven of the Pharisees and Herod" (8:15). There is mounting hostility from official quarters.

Yet there is still hope. It originates in unlikely places, like the case of the blind beggar who comes for Jesus' healing touch (8:22–26). He is restored in two stages, by the application of a "second touch." This second attempt at healing blind people has no parallel in the other Gospels. At first, the man can distinguish objects but they are out of focus and blurred. Then he gets a sharp picture on his retina, as Jesus touches him again.

Mark intends us to see the point as it is applied to the Twelve, who are also blind. They see who Jesus is—but indistinctly and in a hazy way. After the cross, when they finally admit their need, they will get a new understanding.

WHAT DOES IT MEAN TODAY?

There are some central matters in these stories, that hopefully have been illumined in our exposition. I suppose we could sum up the chief thrust in one epigram: *The heart of the "religion" of Jesus is the "religion" of the heart.* Or, more accurately, the inner meaning and motivation is more important than the outward display. We can see this root principle applied in several areas.

1. What exactly was wrong with the Pharisees' religious belief and practice? Jesus put His finger on the partly exposed nerve, in 7:13, "You set aside God's word by your tradition." For them, religion was following a custom; a testy, brittle attitude to observances all intended to keep cultic piety intact—like washing pots and removing specks of dust; and especially a code book creed, where everything is spelled out in the finest of fine print.

Jesus, on the other side, put God's will for human life in its fullness at the top of His list. Obeying God in day-by-day situations is exacting and an adventure. It includes risks! Not everything is black-and-white; there are shaded regions of gray where you need to stop and ask: What would God have me be and do here? The answer usually comes in the call of responsibility to others, especially our family—not very trendy, to be sure, but so relevant today when the rule is: Does it please *me?*

And then, He is more interested in our inner life—the pictures on our mental screen and our character—than with the nice issues of our social mores ("whatever goes into a man," in v. 18). He puts His finger on the real issue: *From within, out of a man's heart* (mind), the real state of a person's life is determined (v. 21).

Words are a sure index. We put our character where our mouth is! (Read again James 3:1–18.)

2. We can so easily categorize people with our handy labels: "Jew *versus* Gentile," as in 7:24–30, which had become, in Jesus' time, more of "specially favored, nice people" *versus* "dirty Gentile dogs."

"The good" and "the bad" are too neat a division, since we are *all* bad in ourselves, and we have nothing but by God's free, unmerited grace—even if we may be white, Anglo-Saxon, and Protestant, with "orthodox" and "holy" thrown in for good measure!

Jesus came to bless people according to their need, not because of racial privileges, or their sex, or their nationality. On these three counts, this person in 7:26 was a born loser. She was a woman (a sad misfortune, in the eyes of the rabbis, all male, of course). She was a Greek (her national status and pagan religion were wrong). She was a Syrophoenician (a member of the wrong race as well). How could she win?

But she did. Not because she was a women, Greek and Syrophoenician but because, out of a deep sense of personal and altruistic need, she came to Jesus—with bold, persistent, perceptive *faith*. And that sort of audacious faith always wins, where Jesus is concerned. (Take a look at Matthew 8:5–13.)

Matthew's version (15:28) is a motto for us all: "O woman, great is your faith! Be it done for you as you desire."

3. A craving for signs (8:11–13) is so natural—to the "natural man" of 1 Corinthians 2:14. It asks to see proofs and demonstrations, courtesy of God Himself. It wants to lean on a crutch before committing oneself to Him in sheer trust, backed only by His promised Word. It proposes to have faith validated in experience *before* it ventures out in full abandon. It seeks some security other than in God alone.

Now, let me ask myself, where is *my* faith directed today? Faith in faith? Faith in experiences? Faith in charismatic signs? Or faith in God?[7]

66

Footnotes

1. This section is like a lengthy footnote, intended to explain Jewish customs for Mark's Gentile readers who would not be familiar with Palestinian ceremonial procedures.

2. A recent archaeological find reveals this word on a box of bones, an ossuary, in Palestine. The inscription declared that the contents, including a man's personal possessions, were dedicated to God, and so removed from profane or common use by the finder.

3. I have considered some of these texts in "Idols, Meat offered to," *New Bible Dictionary*, pp. 554, 555.

4. More details of the Mark-Paul tie-up in Ralph P. Martin, *Mark: Evangelist and Theologian*, pp. 210ff., 220–22.

5. Noted by A. Richardson, *The Miracle Stories of the Gospels*, pp. 97, 98.

6. They were "seeking" (a loaded word in Mark, always implying a threat to Jesus' ministry; see Mark 1 and 3) from Him a sign "from heaven."

7. "Faith ceases to be faith when it clamours for visible or tangible proof," writes Hugh Anderson, *The Gospel of Mark*, p. 199.

Challenges
and
Claims
Mark 8:27—9:8

WHERE ARE WE GOING?

Mark's story of Jesus gives the impression that it contains a lot of separate incidents which are strung together without much connection between them. The reader could easily suppose that this Gospel isn't leading up to a climax, but it is rather concerned just to group stories together by a common interest, such as the mighty works of Jesus in 4:35—5:43. But that would be a wrong impression. There *is* a plan in Mark, even if it is not obvious at first glance.

One of the clearest landmarks is the sign of the cross. Of course, the Passion story in the final chapter (11—15) tells in some detail about the cross where Jesus suffered. Yet it is just as true that the first half of the Gospel also leads up to the plain announcement of the cross.

Mark 8:31-38 is like a watershed. All that has gone before has been leading up to it. All that follows will flow from it. The incident at Caesarea Philippi stands at the center of the Gospel, at a midpoint of the chapters; and it represents Jesus' furthest journey away from Jerusalem and Galilee. After this confrontation at Caesarea Philippi in the northeast of Palestine, and His transfiguration on the slopes of a nearby mountain, He turns southward. He set His face toward Jerusalem for the last week there, and to confront events involving the betrayal, the trial, the ordeal of the cross and the Easter victory.

In 8:27—9:1 we are at the parting of the ways. Henceforth the shadow of His impending destiny to suffer and die will fall ever more deeply across Mark's story page.

WHAT DOES IT SAY?
The Question Jesus Asked/8:27–31

Caesarea Philippi got its name from the honor bestowed on the Roman emperor by Philip, one of the sons of Herod the Great. He refounded the city of Paneion (or Paneas; modern name is Banyas) and called it "Philip's Caesarea" to distinguish it from the larger city of the same name, Caesarea on the Mediterranean coastline. It lay strictly outside of Israel, in pagan territory in which Pan, the god of the fields, was worshiped. Jesus' retirement with the Twelve was intended to get them on their own, and away from the pressures of the crowds.

The disciples have been in Jesus' company for some considerable time. Already they have formed some impression of Him and are wondering secretly just who this person may be. So Jesus' question to them, "Who do men say that I am?" is not one fired out of the blue. They know that there are rumors about Jesus filling the air. He is thought to be a great leader of Israel such as John the Baptist or Elijah come back to life. But Jesus presses the issue: "Who do you say that I am?" Peter is the leader of the group and their spokesman. He confesses for them all, "You are the Christ" —the Messiah.

In Mark's account of this dialogue, Jesus receives the tribute of Peter's statement with a certain indifference and coolness, and He told His disciples to keep His Messiahship under wraps (v. 30). In fact, it is as if Mark intends us to see that Jesus was embarrassed by it. This was a politically loaded title.

Some 50 years or so before Jesus came, the expectation of a Messiah had run high. In *The Psalms of Solomon*, a Pharisee writer expresses the fervent hope that a Messiah, the Lord's anointed, would come to deliver the Jews from the hated Romans and lead the nation in a holy crusade to lift Israel to a place of world dominion and liquidate all Gentile opposition with a blast of fury.

Here are some translated passages from this document to give the flavor of how the Messiah was thought of and what expectations the Jews cherished about Him as the messianic Son of David.

(O God) gird him with strength,
that he may shatter unrighteous rulers,
and may (the Messiah) cleanse Jerusalem from the
Gentiles that trample her down in destruction.

Wisely and righteously let him expel
sinners from the inheritance,
and destroy the sinner's pride
as a potter's vessel,

With a rod of iron may he
break in pieces all their resources.
Let him destroy the lawless Gentiles
by the word of his mouth.

At his rebuke the nations shall
flee from his presence,
and he shall convict sinners
in the thoughts of their hearts,

The Lord himself is his king, the hope of
him who is mighty through his hope in God,
and he will have mercy upon all the nations
that come in fear into his presence,

For he will smite the earth
with the word of his mouth for ever.
He will bless the Lord's people
with wisdom and gladness.

And he himself will be pure from sin
so that he may rule a mighty people.
He will rebuke princes and expel sinners
by the might of his word.

Jesus has no aspiration for Himself of fulfilling any of
these dreams. Nor did the Kingdom of God mean for Him
a new order of society in which the Gentiles would be
consumed and the Jews promoted to being the execution-
ers of His wrath on every other people, especially the Romans.

Earlier He had commanded the demons to keep silence
about Him (3:12). Now He bids the disciples to do the
same—and probably for the same reason. He does not want
a wrong publicity that would inflame popular sentiment if
it were reported widely that the Messiah was here as a
wonder-worker.

Jesus firmly believed in the coming of the divine Kingdom. But it would come *only in God's way and in His time.*
At what point in His ministry He saw a terrifying vision of
the way the rule of God is set up and its method of operation we cannot say. But at Caesarea Philippi the grim truth
gripped and mastered Him. The road to His glory as Messiah in the Kingdom runs by way of the cross. *No cross, no
crown.*

And the only Kingdom He came to establish is one built
on love, just as the setting up of that Kingdom must be by
methods which are God-like. The end of the road was
God's rule over human lives; the way to achieve it was for
Him to accept a destiny of suffering and rejection. So He
utters the plain warning of 8:31: "He taught them that the
Son of man [His own favorite self-description] must suffer
much, be repudiated . . . and be put to death, and after three
days rise again. And he spoke this word plainly."

The Destiny Jesus Accepted/8:32–38

He started to talk of the "Son of man." There are various backgrounds of this term, in the Old Testament and the Jewish literature that grew up between Malachi and Matthew. But in this setting the clearest parallel is Daniel 7. There the Son of man in Daniel 7:13 represents a remnant of faithful Jews who, through suffering and hardship (7:21, 25,26), get vindicated and owned by God and receive a world empire (7:22,27). It is likely that Jesus thought of Himself as this "Son of man," destined to suffer, yet one day to be brought by God out of defeat to triumph. So He foretold in Mark 8:31.

The title "Son of man" stands for a leader and a people, just as a shepherd needs a flock of sheep and a king rules a country. The title also speaks of a group. In this case, it is Jesus plus the Twelve. If Jesus is bound to suffer, the Twelve are involved in it with Him. And that was bad news for them.

Peter once again vocalizes the deep reaction of the band. He can't imagine what "Messiah" has to do with defeat, suffering and death, when it suggests—to him, at least—a glorious figure. And he doesn't like what he hears because suffering will affect him and his fellow-disciples too.

So the debate begins. Peter rebukes Jesus. Jesus rebukes Peter. They are at "cross" purposes, since at the heart of the discussion is the cross. For Peter, the indication that the Son of man will die is unthinkable. For Jesus, it is inevitable.

"Get behind me, Satan" (8:33), spoken to Peter, is a bold rejection of Peter's mistaken idea of a political or revolutionary Messiah. It recalls Matthew 4:10 (the wording is very similar) where Jesus responds to the devil's temptation to "fall down and serve him" in exchange for the promise of becoming the world's great dictator. He refused this role with "Out of the way, Satan." Now He identifies Peter as Satan's mouthpiece and agent, and once more He dismisses Satan's suggestion that comes to Him in Peter's reaction.

Yet Jesus is not facing the cross blindly, as though He

72

had no choice but to accept a cruel, irrational sentence of doom. Since the cross, though it is evil in itself, is His Father's good will, He will gladly accept its shame and set His face to go south to the place of His destiny. He will cast aside Satan's alternative.

Any attempt to short-circuit the plan of God that involves the road to suffering and death is treated as part of "human ideas," not what is in God's mind. And for Jesus, only the latter really counts in His life. "I do always the things that please him" (John 8:29) was His lifelong motto.

But will He go on alone? He spells out the terms of discipleship (8:34–38). To be His loyal follower, the disciple must also accept his place in the "Son of man" and be faithful even if it means death.

Notice how voluntary the call to discipleship is. A person, of his own desire and choice, has to count the cost, and take his stand for Jesus. (See Luke 14:27–33.) This voluntaristic principle explains what "taking up the cross" (8:34) entails. It is hardship we accept (1) as a personal choice, that is, it is not forced upon us, and (2) for Jesus Christ's sake, because of our loyalty to Him. It involves, therefore, saying no to self as part of our total commitment to Him in real life situations.

For us today, "taking up the cross" is a common phrase, and it has lost its grim reality. For us it is a picture of some inconvenience or picayune trial, like a touch of arthritic pain or a grouchy boss. Faced with life's petty annoyances which *can* be frustrating and bothersome, we say, "It's my cross. I'll have to bear it."

For Jesus and the disciples who were only too well aware of "the cross," having seen what the Romans could do to slaves and social misfits on the roadsides of Palestine, this "cross" business was no metaphor. "To carry the cross" means one awful thing. "They were to go to Jerusalem like a procession of condemned criminals with halters round their necks."[1]

Some excellent textual authorities translate verse 38: "Whoever is ashamed *of me and of mine* [i.e., Jesus and the disciples seen as a unit, the corporate Son of man]...."

73

Clearly what is meant is that if Jesus and the Twelve go to Jerusalem to suffer, they will be vindicated by God. If the supporters of Jesus drop out and turn against Him and the disciples, they will be disowned by God. Eventually Jesus was deserted *by all*—the Twelve and the crowd (Mark 14:49)—and left to be Son of man *in His own person.*[2]

The phrase, "When he comes in the glory of his Father with the holy angels" (v. 38, *RSV*), looks ahead to the *parousia*, or presence of Christ in His second advent (see 1 Thess. 4:15–17). This is His coming in glory.

But the disciples to whom He spoke at Caesarea Philippi had a foretaste of this *either* at Pentecost, when He came back in the power of the Spirit *or* at the Transfiguration as they saw Him bathed in the glory that one day will be His, according to Philippians 3:20,21.

The Glory Jesus Displayed/9:1–8

He had spoken about the glory that one day would be His—and theirs, if they were faithful to the end (8:38). But what of the immediate future? Are there no encouragements given to provide strength to face the trials ahead of them?

First, there is the promise of Jesus Himself (9:1), that some of those who were His present disciples would not die until they had seen their faith vindicated and their allegiance to the suffering Christ rewarded. That seems to mean the fulfillment of all that Jesus' passion and triumph would bring at the day of Pentecost, which was the beginning of the new age of world history, as Calvin thought. The risen Lord would show His triumph by sending the Spirit and inaugurating God's Kingdom in the Church. Every Pentecost Christians around the world celebrate the Church's birthday, and the coming of God's Kingdom in power (Acts 1:3–5, 2:33).

But it is just as possible that the fulfillment of 9:1 came a week later after the episode at Caesarea Philippi. Then He climbed with the favored three disciples, Peter, James, and John, to a spur of Mount Hermon (or Tabor).[3] His outer form was dramatically changed and He appeared in the glory that will be His at the end of the age (see 2 Pet. 1:16–19), at His second coming.

Elijah and Moses talked with Jesus (Mark 9:4). The theme of their conversation is given in Luke 9:31; it was His "departure [Greek word is *exodos*] which he was to accomplish at Jerusalem" (*RSV*). The topic was His way of saving the world. But how was that to be achieved? Peter had imagined it could be by force of military strength or by a salvation-without-the-cross. The Hebrew patriarchs knew better.

Peter recognized that Jesus was no military leader or Son of David, but his mind was still full of wrong ideas. What does Peter's suggestion, "Do you wish us to make three tents, one for you, one for Moses and one for Elijah?" (Mark 9:5) mean? It is not easy to say. An attractive possibility is that the mention of "tents" or "booths" has to do with celebration of the Jewish festival of Tabernacles (literally, "Booths") in Judaism (Lev. 23:39–43). Then, as the Jews relived the experience of their fathers throughout their desert wanderings, their nationalistic feelings ran high and their hopes of a political deliverance were raised to fever pitch. Peter is trading on this fact, and by his suggestion that he should erect three booths, he is calling on Jesus to lead the nation (as Moses did) and extricate the oppressed people from their enemies, as Elijah did so victoriously.

My interpretation is that Peter is mentioning to Jesus a quick and easy way to arrive at the "glory" of which He had spoken (8:38). In Jewish literature both Israelite figures, Moses and Elijah, had a splendid exit from this life to the next—and both were spared the pain of suffering and death. (See 2 Kings 2:11 for Elijah's ascension to heaven. The Jewish rabbis believed that Deut. 34:5,6 meant that since God buried him, Moses went home to God in a special way).[4] Peter insinuates, "Step up to glory from the mount—and take us with you to your glorious realm." A rebuke from Jesus seems to precede Peter's statement in verse 6, "*He did not know what he should answer.*" The implication is that Peter had no answer to what Jesus said to him. This rebuke would have been nothing less than Jesus' second word of reproach to poor misguided Peter (see 8:33).

It follows naturally that when the cloud came and obscured them, then took Moses and Elijah away, and the heavenly voice sounded, they expressed surprise that Jesus was still with them (v. 8). He had not gone into heaven. Instead He came down from the mountain, and set His steps on the hard road that would lead to Calvary. That was the way to His glory, and He chose it freely though at the great cost. Read Philippians 2:6–11 for what the choice really meant.

WHAT DOES IT MEAN TODAY?

1. Jesus and Peter are strange partners in a disputation (8:32), and the contest is unequal. It is a foolhardy, brash man who ventures to tell Jesus that He is on the wrong track. So Peter finds himself rebuked for good measure.

What is the issue at stake? Answer: Both men have the same goal and it is altogether good and praiseworthy. Both Jesus and Peter want to see God's rule begin and His dominion accepted in human lives and in the world. But the way to achieve this is different, as the sharp contrast is put in verse 33.

The "thoughts of men" stand over against God's thoughts, with Peter ranged on one side, and Jesus on the other. Here is the stark alternative:

The Kingdoms of the world go by,
In purple and in gold;
They rise, they triumph, and they die,
And all their tale is told.

One Kingdom only is divine,
Its banners triumph still.
Its king a servant, and its sign
A cross upon a hill.

Now the question for us to consider: Which side are we on?

What is our hope for God's rule, and how do we expect to see it established?

2. Peter—poor man once again, really messed up in his thinking—wanted to build three booths (9:5). Irrespective of what they were supposed to represent, it is clear that Peter wanted to put Jesus and Moses and Elijah *on the same level.* [5] He was like a modern professor of comparative religion, for whom all religions are equal, and Jesus is no better than Socrates, Plato, Buddha, or Gandhi. There may be "comparative religions"—but Christianity is not one of them, if we take seriously the New Testament witness to the uniqueness of Jesus Christ, and His unrivaled place in history as the only Son of God in a class of one.

Small wonder that when the cloud wafts away the two Old Testament figures, "Jesus is left alone." That's where He belongs, by right.

Worthy, O Lamb of God, art Thou,
That every knee to Thee should bow.

Footnotes

1. C.H. Dodd, *The Founder of Christianity,* pp. 94, 95.
2. For an exciting exposition of this theme, see T.W. Manson, *The Teaching of Jesus.*
3. The two mountains are connected (see Ps. 89:12).
4. Elijah and Moses were associated in the rabbinic literature with Enoch as "three men who went up alive to heaven," and never tasted the bitterness of death. See Ralph P. Martin, *Mark: Evangelist and Theologian,* pp. 171, 172 for data.
   Moses' burial was a mystery, and what happened to his corpse became the subject of much debate by the Jewish teachers. See Jude 9.
5. See H. Anderson, *The Gospel of Mark,* p. 226.

7
Faith and Failure

Mark 9:9-50

WHERE ARE WE GOING?

The step-up from the mountain of the Transfiguration to our Lord's native heaven would have been easy. One short step and He would have followed the way of other illustrious figures, such as Moses and Elijah—and especially Enoch who was taken up so that he should not see death (Gen. 5:24; Heb. 11:5). But Jesus had no intention of fulfilling the Old Testament Scripture, represented by Moses (the Law) and Elijah (the Prophets) in that easy way. Instead He saw His appointment with destiny in terms of a suffering Son of man. The conversation with the disciples on the path down from the mountain turns on the identity of this Son of man.

WHAT DOES IT SAY?
Jesus and His Destiny/9:9–13

The disciples are genuinely puzzled. They have heard their Master speak of a Son of man who is bound to suffer

(8:31) before He receives God's crown of success and glory (8:38). They have just witnessed the splendid scene on the mountain when Jesus' outer form became dazzlingly resplendent, such as no laundry on earth could bleach and brighten—a vividly expressed detail found only in Mark (9:3).

They have heard the heavenly voice booming out of the cloud, "This is my beloved Son: listen to him," a command given first in the prophecy of Moses that a great prophet who would demand attention would one day appear (Deut. 18:15). Now they are told that Jesus is greater than Moses and comes with a message that supersedes the ancestral faith. The two greatest men in Israel's history retire and disappear, and their Master is left alone, in solitary splendor. All this is great. But there is a snag.

What disturbs them is that He goes on to talk of the Son of man's *rising from the dead.* But if the Son of man is to rise, is He first to die? Yes, He will enter His glory only as He first treads the path of suffering and death. But, they ask, how can this happen? The Son of man is a glorious figure (Dan. 7:13) who is received at the throne of God and there He is crowned with honor.

Jesus answers their objection in three ways. *First,* Daniel's Son of man gets to the throne only along a road of affliction such as faithful Jews were willing to endure in time of fierce persecution.

Second, the Old Testament prophets talk of another figure whose vocation, given Him by God, is to suffer on His people's behalf. (Mark 8:31 and 9:31 clearly indicate a destiny of suffering followed by vindication as God steps in to reverse the verdict of men and exalt Jesus to the glory of His presence.) This is the suffering servant of Isaiah 53. Verse 12 in our passage relates the suffering of the Son of man to Isaiah's prophecy by using terms first found in Isaiah 52:13—53:12.

The prophecy that Elijah will come back to prepare for the Messiah stems from Malachi 4:5. Jesus identifies Elijah with John, and goes on to make the point that this time Elijah has suffered a cruel fate (see Mark 6:17–29).

Third, if the disciples had the wit to see it, Jesus' commitment to suffering has already been dramatized before their eyes. John the Baptist, as the second Elijah, has come—and gone by way of a martyr's death. He came to prepare Jesus' way, not only in being a forerunner but, more significantly, in setting a pattern of suffering unto death that Jesus sees as His destiny too. Only His death will save the world, because He is the "greater one" John foretold (1:7). Nonetheless, John was not like Elijah who escaped the wrath of his enemies. He met his fate head-on. The Son of man can expect no less (9:12).

Jesus and the Disciples' Failure/9:14–16,28–50

All these passages should be read together. They are joined together by a common theme. The chosen Twelve, whom Jesus called to be with Him (3:13–19) and whom He sent out as His representatives (6:7–13) were in a special position to observe Him at close quarters and to appreciate who He was. Peter had hailed Him as God's royal Man, the Messiah come to set God's people free. Three of them had had unique privileges. They had witnessed His glory on the mount and had received the Father's message. Yet, when they are put to the test, they miserably fail. Let us notice the areas of their weakness, and set down what all this means for us today:

1. At the time when the nine disciples at the base of the mountain were approached by the man whose son was demented, there was an argumentative spirit which betrayed a lack of faith (9:16,19) and discipline (vv. 28,29). The disciples admit to their failure which is only too apparent. The sad word of the boy's father is, "I asked your disciples to drive out the evil spirit, but they couldn't." Evidently they had tried but failed.

And this was a cause of contention among them (v. 16) as Jesus realized that they were wrangling among themselves; perhaps He overheard their loud, strident voices in heated discussion. Jesus uttered one of His most poignant, heartrending cries, "O unbelieving race of men, how long shall I be with you? How long do I have to put up with you?" What caused Him this grief was the disciples' failure to express their faith through prayer and fasting as we read from verses 28,29 in the "post mortem" rap session He held with them after He had taken control of the situation.

2. The same men were still in doubt over Jesus' purpose. When He taught them plainly, and for the second time, that He came to die, they shake their heads in total and uncomprehending dismay (vv. 30–32).

3. They still cherish ambitious plans for their individual greatness. On the road that would lead their Master to His cross, their minds are filled with thoughts of "who is the best among us?" Jesus gives them an object lesson of a little child (vv. 33–37). Only the childlike spirit—one of lowliness, trustfulness, and unself-conscious simplicity—gets to understand God's Kingdom, as Jesus will teach in 10:13–16.

4. It is almost inevitable that a proud, self-assertive attitude displayed by the Twelve will lead to a haughty exclusivism which looks down on those around them, especially the exorcism-practicing man who claimed to be engaged in the service of Jesus, but who did not belong to their "group." The disciple John is the tragic spokesman for all in the later Church who imagine that only they are right and only they know what true success is in the Lord's work. Read 9:38–41 as Jesus' rebuke of such a narrow, sectarian spirit.

5. Finally, the disciples were in danger, not only of betraying such a woeful misunderstanding of Jesus, but— more seriously—of leading others astray (vv. 42–50). In this context the "little one" of verse 42 may be the "man casting out demons" of verse 38.

The cruel and unusual punishment of death by drowning with a millstone fastened around a person's neck was suffered by Jewish freedom-fighters, the Zealots, in the first uprising against Rome in A.D. 6, according to the Roman historian Suetonius; Josephus, *Antiquities* XIV, XV, 10, refers to this practice also. Jesus is using this well-known fact as a solemn warning of a fearful (spiritual) penalty to be meted out to those who lead other believers astray.[1]

If the reference to the millstone is understood as "picture language," though it is still terribly real and meaningful, we should interpret "Gehenna" (Mark 9:43) in the same way. Gehenna (literally, "valley of Hinnom") was a ravine south of Jerusalem and used as the city trash disposal center. The rubbish was burned here, and so the place acquired a reputation as a place of destruction, and of the punishment of sinners in the future life.

Jesus' warnings are meant to shake His hearers' complacency. They were thinking, "The Gentiles will burn in hell"; Jesus turned it around, "You will suffer and die in an awful place like Gehenna if you fail to heed my words and if you live careless lives that prove a hindrance to other people."

"Salted with fire" (v. 49) is probably a proverb. No reference to purgatory in the next world is intended. The thought is rather that, as salt purifies, so Christians who face suffering, as in Nero's outburst against the Church in Mark's day, will be tested.

In this section Jesus makes it plain that giving some weak, faltering, inexperienced disciple a hard time will be treated by Him as serious. Some of His most searching words were spoken to leaders who put stumbling blocks in the path of other people. No amount of zeal and earnestness for the truth can compensate for a careless attitude and uncharitable judgment that would cause young Christians to miss the right road because the professed followers of Jesus set them such a poor example.

Jesus and Faith's Shining Example/9:19–27

If we are challenged by the disciples' sad failures, we are encouraged by the father's glad response. This snatch of dialogue is one of the most graphic and lifelike in the entire Gospel. Read it in a modern translation, and it really comes alive.

We pick up the story of the father's need. Jesus is in command of the situation as He comes on the scene. And He asks that the sick boy be brought to Him. The boy is in great distress. His complaint is long-standing, his symptoms are distressing, and there is no apparent hope. Even Jesus' disciples, trying their hand at exorcism, find this a hard case.

But there is one redeeming feature to brighten the gloomy scene. The father's heart-cry is, "If you can do anything, have pity on us and help us" (v. 22, *RSV*). Jesus sees the glimmer of faith and picks up the father's phrase: "Did you say, 'If you can?' Why, everything can be done for anyone who has faith." The response is, "I do have faith. Help me in the little faith I have." That's all Jesus needs to come to his aid.

As with the story in Matthew 8:5–13, the presence of a positive faith-attitude moves Him to action, and releases His mighty power. He was amazed at faith's absence at Nazareth (Mark 6:6); He is thrilled at faith's presence here, and He quickly responds. So it is today, as we ask what the story has to say to us when we read it. What Jesus looked for long ago and still looks for in us is *faith*—even "little faith" which can grow.

Faith, mighty faith, the promise sees,
And looks to that alone;
Laughs at impossibilities,
And cries: It shall be done!
                              Charles Wesley
Lord, I believe, Help me in my weak faith.

WHAT DOES IT MEAN TODAY?

The vivid narrative of the possessed boy, his father and the disciples' failure spotlights the nature of *faith*.

"Faith," says J. Alexander Findlay, "as illustrated in Mark's Gospel, may be defined as a painstaking and concentrated effort to obtain blessing for oneself or for others, material or spiritual, inspired by a confident belief that God in Jesus can supply all human need."[2]

The vignette in 9:14–27 tells us several things about faith:

1. It sets forth Jesus as the Man of faith, the great example of the perfect Believer. This, I suggest, is how we should read verses 22,23.

Father: "Your disciples cannot do anything to help us. If you can do anything, please do it."

Jesus: "Do I hear you say, 'If you can?' I tell you, everything can be done for the person who has faith in God, and I am that person, since I trust my Father to do what you need. Why don't you trust Him too, like me? Come, share my faith in God."

2. Faith often is exposed to trial and testing. (see 1 Pet. 1:6,7). The father's cry in response is, "I do believe." No doubt he thought all was well at that point and that his son would be instantaneously healed that very moment. If so, he was in for a rude shock.

Read verses Mark 9:25,26. Jesus rebuked the demon. It threw the lad into convulsions and he lay rigid. People began to murmur, "He's dead. Jesus has killed him." How dreadful the father must have felt at this agonizing moment. "I asked Jesus to help. Now my boy is dead." But that wasn't the end. Jesus raised him, and "all's well that ends well!" The man's faith was honored, but not before it was sorely tested and shaken. Exactly true to life, isn't it?

3. The discipline of faith is taught in verse 29. Nothing comes easily, not even faith. Simple, naive "believism" is a sham and a phony. *Faith is God's free gift, but it's not cheap.* We have to exercise faith, cultivate it, live by it—and promote its growth by "prayer and fasting." A tenacious faith is great, but we have to work at it, and allow nothing to impede: No negligence, no careless attitudes, no false security, no dallying with sin.

So, "make your calling and election sure" (2 Pet. 1:10, *KJV*) by living a true life in which profession and practice go hand in hand.

Footnotes
1. Jesus spoke most of His terrifying words about hell as a warning to His professed followers. See W. Strawson, *Jesus and the Future Life.*
2. J.A. Findlay, *Jesus as They Saw Him,* p. 107.

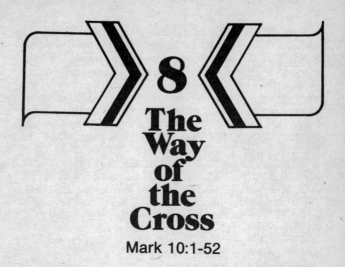

8

The Way of the Cross

Mark 10:1-52

WHERE ARE WE GOING?

Luke's Gospel has a section (extending from 9:51 to 18:14 or 19:44) which is often called the Travel Narrative. This is because it begins with the notice that Jesus set His face to go up on the road to Jerusalem to meet His rendezvous with destiny there (Luke 9:51). Thereafter He continues on the road that will bring Him to the holy city (Luke 13:22; 17:11).

Mark is not so interested in this travel section. But he is clear that, once Jesus had received the disciples' confession at Caesarea Philippi (Mark 8:27–30), He began to teach them plainly about His sacrifice. It is understood that the sacrifice could only be made at Jerusalem as He makes it clear in 10:33. His story moves inexorably from Galilee by way of the right bank of the Jordan River on to Judea—and Jerusalem. The journey begins at 10:1.

What Mark lacks in precise geographical detail, he makes up for in vivid narrative and arresting word pictures. Read 10:32 for what is surely the most gripping piece of vigorous writing in the entire Gospel. It is a scene worthy of the artist's canvas and brush. The Twelve and Jesus are on the road to Jerusalem. Jesus is striding ahead of them, as though He wants to make all speed, while they lag behind. They are amazed at His eagerness to press forward, yet they follow Him even if fear grips them. They are fearful because of the uncertainty of what lies ahead. He is courageous and confident because He knows that only in Jerusalem can the Father's will and purpose be worked out, even though it involves His suffering and death (10:32–34).

Let us use this one expression—"Jesus on the road," which runs like a thread to bind together the various incidents in chapter 10—as a key to the whole.

WHAT DOES IT SAY?
Jesus on Marriage/10:1–12

Jesus' Galilean ministry is over, and He is heading south to Judea. As He sets foot on Judean soil, a fresh conflict breaks out. The point at issue is the vexed question of marriage and divorce. Jewish law in regard to divorce was based on the interpretation of Deuteronomy 24:1. Divorce is permitted if a man, having married a women, finds a "shameful thing" (literally, "nakedness of a thing") in her. For the rabbis the question centered on what exactly made a wife's conduct improper and so suitable as grounds of a divorce action on the man's part.

Notice that Jewish law did not permit a wife to initiate divorce proceedings against her husband for *his* misconduct. Her only way to gain release from the marriage bond was to persuade her husband to take the initiative and let her go free.

The point in verse 2 is that Jesus is again put on the spot—or so His enemies imagine. They want Him to give a ruling on Deuteronomy 24:1 and to say what His interpretation of "a shameful thing" is. Several facets of the subject were covered by His reply.

86

1. He declared, in effect, that any kind of divorce is "a shameful thing," since Moses' permission is only second-best in any case. God's original intention, declared in His paradise-ordinance (Gen. 2:24), is that marriage is a partnership for all time, involving a lifelong commitment on both sides and is not to be broken (so Mark 10:6,7,9: What God has joined together, let not man [i.e. Moses' law] separate).

2. For Jesus, this kind of marriage is an equal partnership, in which husband and wife stand together before God. He is challenging the obviously unfair situation in which the man has rights of divorce which the woman does not have. This was Jesus' new teaching, expressed in verse 12.

3. His teaching is that divorce followed by remarriage with a third party runs counter to God's purpose (vv. 10–12).[1]

4. Basic in Jesus' teaching is His claim to bringing in the age of the Messiah that supersedes the age of Moses, by fulfilling the law.

Jesus on the Nature of God's Kingdom/10:13–31

Mark's Gospel opens with the theme of God's Kingdom soon to be set up. The first word Jesus ever uttered in public promised that the Kingdom—God's rule over human lives in an ideal society—was near (1:14,15). His parables (Mark 4) were all about the Kingdom's presence and power. Yet there was misunderstanding, as we shall see. Mark intends us to observe in 10:13–16 those who really illustrate the sort of people that can enter God's realm.

The Kingdom belongs to the childlike. If we take a starting point in the fact that, on the eve of *Yom Kippur* (the Day of Atonement, when Israel mourned for her national sins each October), children were brought to Jewish rabbis for blessing, it may well be that this is the key to the passage. The parents understand what Jesus' purpose is all about. He makes these little ones a special object lesson: "Of such as these"—whose lives are a continual "Day of Atonement" since they are all the time conscious of their needs and weaknesses—"is the Kingdom of God."[2]

87

Jesus taught childlikeness as a human trait, not childishness. What makes children so apt an illustration is not their innocence, but their simplicity, gratitude and trustfulness. Little ones do not expect anything from their parents on the score of merit or as a reward. They are helpless, and so they are utterly dependent.

If we turn it around, Jesus' teaching is forceful and direct. Nothing bars the entrance to the Kingdom so effectively as self-trust and pride in one's attainments, just as no attitude so commends us to God as one of helpless committal.

The Kingdom is not for those secure in their riches. On the negative side, we see in 10:17–27 how people fail to make it to God's Kingdom. This story is the exact opposite of the one in which children are blessed. A rich man came running—an unusual feature, since few people ran under the hot Palestinian sun—and wanted a quick answer to a profound question.

"Good Teacher," he asks, "what must I do to inherit eternal life?" (v. 17, *RSV*).

Jesus' reply, "Why do you call me good?" was not meant to deny that title to Himself but to sober the questioner. The man ran up with a flattering remark to gain Jesus' approval. Jesus asks him to think about his language. Does he really know what "goodness" is? Only one person is perfect goodness and that person is God. Religious titles and religious terms are not to be used as ploys to ingratiate the speaker.

Jesus continues to search out his motives. Has he kept the commandments? Yes, comes back the response, all except where it really counts. He is a moral and well-adjusted individual, but Jesus says, "You lack one thing." He is still self-sufficient and his trust is in his possessions. Riches are not evil *per se*. But they can so easily become the object of trust.

Mammon means "wealth." It is derived from a Hebrew verb *Amen* meaning "to trust," "to confide in." We see this whenever we make a response to a prayer with a spoken declaration of "amen"—"I believe," "I confirm." So Jesus uttered one of His most challenging words: "You cannot serve God and mammon" (Matt. 6:24, *RSV*) because trust in one excludes trust in the other.

This is the root problem with the ruler: He needs to let go of the obstacle that stops his commitment to God in full trust. In his case it was his money. So Jesus called him to sell all, give it to the needy, and then to come and join His band of committed men.

The challenge was too much, because the wealthy man loved his possessions, and he went away with a clouded face. The story illustrates exactly Paul's definition: "Covetousness"—love of money for its own sake—"is idolatry" (Col. 3:5). The rich man had so much in his favor. In fact, he had too much, and consequently he lacked a sense of need. Without that awareness of our desperate condition we will never come to Christ and appreciate His grace. (See Rev. 3:17–19 for professed Christians who are saying in their pride, "I am rich, I have prospered. I have no need of anything.") The young ruler trusted in his riches, and his gold and his goods became his gods. Nobody gets to heaven when his hands are full of his merits and achievements, said Jesus.

The disciples are puzzled (Mark 10:28–31) because, in the Old Testament, riches are a sign of God's favor. In the New Testament, they are often a barrier to faith, for the reasons given in 10:23–27. The rich person finds it hard to enter God's Kingdom.

To get a camel (the largest animal in Palestine) to pass through the eye of a needle (the smallest aperture the Jews could think of) is to attempt the impossible. Just so, says Jesus, using this current proverb, it is absurd to try to enter the door of the Kingdom with a huge bag of wealth strapped to one's person. "How hard it is for them that trust in riches to enter into the kingdom of God!" (v. 24, *ASV*). This idea is strikingly endorsed in 1 Timothy 6:6–11,17–19.

"Then who can be saved?" the disciples ask incredulously. "All things are possible with God" (Mark 10:27, *RSV*), Jesus replies. All hope of salvation rests on God, as He told Abraham (Gen. 18:14). What no human being achieves by merit or strength, He can accomplish in grace.

Note how in the list of spiritual enrichments of life that come to the disciples (Mark 10:29–31) is added the reminder, "together with persecutions." This grimly realistic note is struck only in Mark's Gospel, as though to emphasize to His suffering Church that afflictions and hardships for Christ's sake must be expected.

Jesus on the Kingdom/10:32–45

This section is the third and final prediction of the Passion, and it is the most detailed. Jerusalem is set as the final destination of the journey (v. 32). The reason for this is given in Luke 13:33: "I must go on my way [to Jerusalem] . . . ; for it cannot be that a prophet should perish away from Jerusalem" (*RSV*). He sets His face to the last, fateful journey toward the holy city, and to His rendezvous with destiny.

"The objective is to be Jerusalem; and to go to Jerusalem is to face a violent death."[3]

Mark's account of this Passion prediction holds nothing back in terms of the horror and indignity that will await Jesus (Mark 10:33,34). We can hardly believe that, with these somber scenes of mockery, disgrace and physical beating realistically painted, the disciples could be so obtuse and unfeeling as the next episode describes them (10: 35–45).

James and John, two of the three privileged disciples (in 5:37; 9:2), come to Jesus with a request, "Let us sit one on your right side and one on your left side in your glory." (To be seated in this way was a mark of honor and special favor, according to 1 Kings 2:19 and Josephus, *Antiquities*, VI, XI, 9.)

They want ringside seats in the extravaganza that they expect to witness in Jerusalem. They hope Jesus will enter the city in triumph and be hailed as a glorious success. They want to be sure that they share it with Him. The other 10 disciples are highly indignant at this—not that they think differently, but because James and John have "jumped the line" and got their applications in first.

Jesus has to clear away these misunderstandings. His

reply to this request is to promise only what can be granted: a share in His baptism. This is a picture of a very real experience, closely linked with drinking a cup (of suffering).

"To drink a cup" is common in the Old Testament for an experience of misery and woe, sometimes involving divine judgment (Ps. 75:8; Isa. 51:17f.; Jer. 49:12; Lam. 4:21; Ezek. 23:31f.). There are also passages in the Old Testament that describe a person's happiness and prosperity under the figure of "drinking a cup" (Ps. 16:5; 23:5; 116: 13). Yet the dominant note is sounded in the somber tones of suffering.

Jesus described His forthcoming death as a baptismal experience (Luke 12:50), looking forward to Gethsemane and Golgotha. The thought of baptism—"being drowned in deep waters"—suggests the experience of being plunged under waters of grief and anguish (see Pss. 42:7; 69:2,15; 124:4,5; Isa. 43:2).

For the Jew in Jesus' day, baptism was a token of God's renewal of His people as a prelude to the coming of the Kingdom. The Dead Sea Scrolls speak of baptismal washings which those at Qumran practiced as a method of purifying by the Holy Spirit (1 QS 4) so that they would be ready to greet the arrival of God's rule in their midst. Maybe John and James thought that this is what their Master had in view: "Come, share my 'baptism' as we together get ready in Jerusalem to see God's Kingdom come." And "drinking the cup" may have suggested a festivity and a celebration in Jerusalem.

If this is what they thought, they were grossly mistaken. Their error was the persistent one, made by Peter in Mark 8:29,31–33, of imagining that the time of messianic blessedness could come any other way than by the "suffering of the Messiah," i.e., involving Jesus and the Twelve.

So James and John replied affirmatively in 10:39, only to be rebuked by Jesus in the next verse, even as He predicts that they are destined to suffer with Him in due course. They failed Him as he approached Calvary (see 14:50), but when the perfect offering had been made by Jesus alone, they took their place in the noble army of martyrs—James by suffering a violent death (Acts 12:2) and John by being exiled for his faith on Patmos (Rev. 1:9).

There will be no glory without suffering, just as there is no meaning of the Kingdom except that this truth sinks in these men's minds: The rule of God is built on redemption. And redemption comes through suffering. The Son of man has His title to Lordship in a ministry of service to God and men and of suffering to atone for sins.

In verses 42–45 we come close to entering the full meaning of what Jesus meant by discipleship. He Himself set the pattern in the memorable lines of verse 45: The Son of man did not come to be served but to serve and to give His life as the ransom price for His people's sins. Jesus' whole ministry is epitomized in this text, which recalls Isaiah 53.

Above all, He is the slave (Greek *doulos* is more emphatic than *diakonos*, "servant" in v. 45). So He calls His followers to tread in His path, by finding that the way to Lordship is not one we grasp at by asserting our rights and bossing others about. It is quite different from the lordship concept in the surrounding Roman and Jewish world where "might is right," and bosses and tin-gods lord it over their underlings (v. 42).

In Jesus' company the title to greatness is given to the person who serves other people most (v. 43), just as Jesus is now Lord of all because He first humbled Himself and took the part of a slave (Greek *doulos*), according to Philippians 2:6–8. On that basis, Paul encourages us: "Let this mind be yours" (Phil. 2:5).

The background to 10:45, the so-called "ransom saying," was the current Jewish idea that atonement from wrong could be achieved by four methods: repentance, sacrifice, suffering, and death. The martyrs in Israel's history were thought of as dying for others within the nation, and a condemned criminal was invited, before his execution, to confess that his death put away all his sins.

In addition to Isaiah 53, the setting just given helps us to understand Jesus' way of calling His death a ransom and atonement. But there are obvious differences. He is not dying for His own sins. On the contrary, He is dying for others. And these include "the many" (spoken of in Isa. 52:14; 53:12), that is, the Gentiles for whom in Judaism there was no hope. This is the surprising outreach in Jesus' mission and work of atonement. He is contemplating above all else a salvation that embraces "the nations" in its scope. As servant of God His death has "unlimited power to atone" for human sins, as J. Jeremias puts it.[4]

Jesus' ministry will climax in His death. But it has been going on long before He reaches the cross. His whole life has been one of submission to the Father's will revealed in Scripture and one of self-giving to others—the poor, the needy, the outcast, and the sinner. "I serve" (see Luke 22:27) has been His motto all the time.

The follower of Jesus can know who Jesus is as he or she catches this spirit. So the disciples are not only woefully mistaken about the reason for His march on Jerusalem. They have missed the reason why He called them to follow Him in the beginning (1:16–20; 3:13–19). In His Kingdom there are no "first places" or grandstand seats or titles of honor. Quite the opposite. True glory is in humble service to others who cannot reward us. The "first place" is at the back, in some obscure situation which only God sees. Real power is exercised in submission to God's loving design for our lives and a willingness to yield our rights, just like a slave (10:43) who has no rights at all.

Jesus is teaching a new ethic as well as explaining the only basis for a person's relationship to God. The cross is *both* the foundation of our hope as sinners *and* the lifestyle of the believer in his dealings with other folk. That's what is meant in the saying, We are saved by two crosses: Christ's cross that atones, and our own that we take up as His followers (8:34).[5]

Jesus on What He Came to Do/10:46–52

All "on the road" is not deep and unrelieved gloom. A shaft of light pierces the darkness of misunderstanding and ignorance. The disciples may have hard hearts and clouded minds (6:51,52). But unlikely people in unlikely places get the message and act upon it. One of Mark's leading themes is just this: *Faith appears in situations where you least expect it,* as we have seen from the story of the Syrophoenician woman (7:24–30) and the distracted father of the paraplegic boy (9:14–27).

Blind Bartimaeus is a nobody on the road of life. His persistent call, "Jesus, Son of David, have pity on me," is an embarrassment to everyone, and they try to hush him. "Don't you know that Jesus has important business on hand? He can't be bothered with wayside beggars," they might have said as they tried to check him from calling out (10:48).

But Jesus had no more pressing concern than with such a man. Like a child, Bartimaeus was poor, wretched, blind and helpless (see again Rev. 3:17–19 which gives a truer assessment of these Christians' real condition from the risen Lord's perspective). But he did have one asset—a confidence in Jesus who, as Messiah, had come to open blind eyes (Isa. 35:5). So he cries out, and he is heard.

Faced with a blank check, "What do you wish me to do for you?" Bartimaeus expresses his obvious desire to get his sight back. Observe his title for Jesus, "Rabboni"—dear Master, exactly like Mary's address in John 20:16. This expressed his personal faith, as Jesus so called it (v. 52) and then honored it. This is a fine example of "insight"-ful faith, that is, Bartimaeus has insight even when he has no eyesight.

What the sophisticated religious people miss, and the privileged disciples pass over as trivial, is the real thing for Jesus. People in need matter. Live faith works. Expectancy gets its reward (10:51).

A poor, wretched outcast gets the message of who Jesus is—the Master of men's lives. He calls out in simple faith and then follows Jesus "on the way" (v. 52) of true discipleship. Mark's readers too would see the significance of "on the road" at the tailpiece of the story.

Jesus must have felt that it *was* worthwhile after all, as He trod the way uphill on the road from Jericho to Jerusalem, and the even steeper, more rugged road up to Calvary where He would meet another wretched man in his need (Luke 23:39–43).

WHAT DOES IT MEAN TODAY?

This passage has been full of lessons of a practical kind, so further comment is not really required. Only our laying the matters to heart, and putting them into practice in our lives! Let's face some single verses, and put a question to ourselves as we read them.

1. "God made them male and female" (Gen. 1:27 which Jesus quotes as authoritative Scripture in Mark 10:6). This teaches the distinctiveness of the sexes. *Vive la différence!* But read on: "The two shall become one flesh" (Gen. 2:24). Here is the fulfillment that marriage brings: each for the other, and both complete in God.

If I'm married, or look forward to marriage: Is my marriage union a partnership in two directions—partner with my spouse, partner with my Creator?

2. "Let the children come to me" (10:14). "Don't stop them." Is there any Christian service more rewarding—in the home, the day school or the Sunday School class than to take Jesus' promise and invitation *seriously*, and encourage our children to find in Him their Saviour and Friend?

3. "One thing you lack" (10:21). In the story, what the young man lacked was courage to deal with an idol, in his case, it was money. In my life, what is it that keeps me back from a full commitment to Christ and His cause?

"Come, follow me"—but only if you mean business with Jesus. "The kingdom of heaven," said James Denney, "is not for the well-meaning; it is for the desperate!" How much in earnest am I when it comes to following Jesus?

He ran up to Jesus, but he went away with leaden feet. Better if he had come thoughtfully, humbly, deliberately; then, he might have gone on his way rejoicing, like someone else did (see Acts 8:39).

4. James and John came with a request that turned out to be both foolish and selfish (10:35). Bartimaeus waited until Jesus asked him what his request was (10:51). Perhaps in this contrast there are two types of praying:

Is my praying, "Give me," "Grant me," "Let me be" somebody important, or useful, or successful in business or church life? Or, do I wait in my Lord's presence until He sees my real condition and then asks me what it is I truly need?

Footnotes

1. For further details, see Ralph P. Martin, *Mark: Evangelist and Theologian*, p. 221.
2. J. Jeremias, *Infant Baptism in the First Four Centuries*, pp. 49f.
3. C.H. Dodd, *The Founder of Christianity*, p. 139.
4. J. Jeremias, *New Testament Theology*, Vol. 1, p. 299.
5. This idea may be the explanation of a problem text in Mark. According to 9:1, Jesus may well have meant: "Among those here present there are some who would never be willing to die before the end of the world, who avoid taking risks, so that they may be alive to see the great Day come." The saying is more an ironical comment than a promise. See E. Trocmé, *The Formation of the Gospel According to Mark*, p. 123.

9
Jesus and His Critics
Mark 11:1—12:44

WHERE ARE WE GOING?

Every great person in the world's history has had friends —and enemies. Even the best of men and women have stirred up opposition and found that there were ranged against them those who envied them or sought to discredit them or made life difficult for them. Jesus was no exception.

We are familiar with the traditional phrase, "scribes and Pharisees," whom Jesus labeled "hypocrites." (Matt. 23 is full of these judgmental words.) Then, there were the Sadducees who also plotted His downfall. And the Romans carried out the grim sentence of death by crucifixion. These were the enemies of Jesus, as everyone knows. But it is a worthwhile question to ask *why* these men opposed Him. Today's passages will give some clues. And these clues are in the shape of action and reaction. Jesus acted in a certain way—by His deeds, His words, His attitudes. His enemies didn't like any of what they saw, heard and understood. So they reacted negatively to Him and the claims He made for Himself.

WHAT DOES IT SAY?
Jesus Claims to Be Lord of the Temple/11:1–19

There were many reasons for what is called the Triumphal Entry into Jerusalem, which is dated on the Sunday before the cross, and which later was called Palm Sunday. For one thing, He provided His disciples with an object lesson in humility. If that is true, we may seriously question whether "*triumphal*" entry is the right word. The disciples may have hoped that it would be so, but Jesus downplayed the "triumph" and rode on a lowly donkey.

The choice of an unbroken animal (11:2) was probably intentional. Beasts that were not yet domesticated were used for religious purposes, such as the oxen chosen to carry back the ark (1 Sam. 6:7; 2 Sam. 6:1–11) and the ceremonial of the red heifer (Num. 19:2; Deut. 21:3). If the young colt was restive when it was submitted to a harness, this would explain why the second animal—the colt's mother—was led alongside. But this is in Matthew's account (21:2–7), not Mark's.

The riding into Jerusalem from the Mount of Olives is full of symbolism as well as of deep historical interest. Doubtless the disciples were still thinking in terms of His march on Jerusalem as a grand entrance of the messianic warrior prince, astride a war horse, conquering and to conquer. Instead, He chose the ass as a lowly beast of burden, and at the same time He fulfilled the Old Testament prediction (Zech. 9:9) He came into Jerusalem in the guise of an unpretentious pilgrim.

It would be wrong to think that Jesus rode in as king, as though He were staging a demonstration to make clear His messianic claims. Decisively against this notion of the Triumphal Entry as a protesters' demonstration is the fact that neither the Jews nor the Romans found it needful to take action against what happened. The incident happened without any official intervention, so it is clear that no claim to being a king, whether overt or secret, was taken as such by the authorities who had tender susceptibilities where mass rallies involving a pretended king were concerned. The Romans put down such a demonstration in A.D. 6 when Judas protested the census, and they did it with a bloody reprisal. (Read Acts 5:36,37.)

Possibly the crowd had other ideas. The starting point from the Mount of Olives—the Hill of Oil as it is called—may have aroused ideas and hopes that this was to be the entry of the Lord's Anointed, based on the popular view that Messiah would stand on this site (Zech. 14:4). The cry of "Hosanna" (meaning "Save now, we pray") expressed a desire for political liberation, according to some interpreters. Quite likely too these cries were an embarrassment to Him.

Then, with the foliage and leafy branches wafted in mid-air as at Tabernacles Feast (Lev. 23:40) as a sign of nationalist fervor, it could be that the crowd was imploring Jesus to do an act of political emancipation and, following in the footsteps of Judas Maccabeus, to cleanse the Temple and restore it to its ceremonial purity by kicking out the Romans. This hope is what the crowd was looking for in their shout, "Blessed is the coming kingdom of our father David" (v. 10).

It is crystal clear that Jesus had no intention of playing the role of liberator nor of repeating the Maccabean crusade by force of arms. His mission was to cleanse the Temple, but His idea of cleansing the Temple was (1) to rid it of *Jewish* defilements and (2) to restore it to its use as a place of worship *for the Gentiles*.

As His first act, Jesus cleared out the merchandising that was going on there, and prohibited anyone from using the Court of the Gentiles as a shortcut across the Temple mount. He declared that this was a sacred enclosure for prayer, open to anyone, non-Jews as well as Jews. The commercial traffic was preventing this. So He put a stop to it, and sanitized the court. Moreover, since all sacrificial offerings had to be paid for in a special Temple coinage, the people were compelled to exchange their Roman currency for the currency in which the Sadducees, the wealthy aristocratic nobility in Jerusalem, traded. These Sadducees were financial officials who held the purse strings. They kept the exchange business firmly under control, and made a fat profit out of it.

Mark's quotation from Isaiah 56:7 clearly explains Jesus' perspective: "My house shall be called a house of prayer *for all nations/Gentiles.*" (The last few words are not in the other evangelists' accounts.)[1] The point of the extended quotation is well brought out by C.H. Dodd, "The Son of David was popularly expected to 'cleanse Jerusalem from the Gentiles' [Psalms of Solomon]. Jesus wanted it cleansed *for* the Gentiles."[2]

When Jesus struck a blow for Gentile privileges which the use of the Court of Gentiles as a stock market and bureau of exchange was denying to them, He was also aiming a shaft at Sadducean prerogative and profit. And they didn't like that any more than their being called keepers of a "den of robbers" (11:17) or maybe a Zealot hideout.

Although Jesus' actions must have got under the skin of the Jewish authorities who saw and heard Him, they couldn't find any criminal activity in either area and they allowed Him to do what He did unmolested.

Jesus and the Fig Tree/11:12–14, 20–26

The next day Jesus was engaged in teaching a message heavy with doom and judgment. The blasting of the fig tree is a difficult incident, since it involves Jesus dealing destructively with a natural object. Some people say that this is unlike His general attitude, and they dismiss the account as an invention.

But that is too hasty. All interpreters agree that this incident is an acted parable or prophetic sign, such as the Old Testament prophets performed to illustrate and drive home their message (see, for instance, Jer. 19 and Ezek. 4,5). The fig tree is the nation of Israel (Hos. 9:10,16; Mic. 7:1–6; Jer. 8:13; 29:17). The destroying of a tree whose leafless condition showed that it was dead or dying is spoken of as an act of judgment (Hos. 2:12; Isa. 34:4). What Jesus is doing is pronouncing on the already sealed fate of the nation. Victor of Antioch, the earliest fifth century commentator on the Gospel of Mark, first expressed this view: Jesus "used the fig tree to set forth the judgment that was about to fall on Jerusalem."[3]

The problem lies (1) in verse 13 with its notice that 'it was not the season for figs' and (2) in Jesus' words recorded in verse 14 when they are understood to be a curse.

Regarding verse 13, figs do not ripen as early as March–April, the Passover season, so how did Jesus expect to find edible fruit when He came from Bethany and was hungry? Possibly there is a veiled scriptural allusion in the parenthesis (so says Lane) or the incident should be dated at Tabernacles set in the previous year.[4]

The difficulty of Jesus' words sounding like a curse (v. 14) is eased once we remember that in Jesus' spoken language of Aramaic the same wording can be taken as a curse, "May no one ever eat fruit from you again"; or as a simple statement of fact, "No one will ever again eat from you." Quite likely, then, Jesus intended a plain declaration. But the disciples thought it was a curse, and so recalled it (as in 11:21).

Either way, we should not miss the sadness in Jesus' words. He is lamenting over the sorry condition of His nation that is bent on despising God's gracious purpose and will inevitably suffer for it in the fall of Jerusalem in A.D. 70.

Jesus and the Pharisees/11:27–33

When Jesus returns to Jerusalem, He is confronted once again by the Pharisees. The issue turns on the central question in all discussions about religion. It comes up in any conversation about God, Christ, the Bible, life after death. Where is true authority to be found? So the Pharisees, who were the professional theologians and doctors of divinity in the Jewish church as well as the leaders in the political community of Israel, put Him on the spot: "By what authority are you doing these things?" (11:28, *RSV*).

101

What things? Mark doesn't tell us, but he leaves us to infer that it was His actions in clearing the Temple courts. Another suggestion is that the dispute was centered on Jesus' baptizing (as in John 3:22–25).[5]

The Pharisee leaders cannot understand why Jesus permits His disciples to baptize (John 4:2) and they recall that Jesus' cousin, John, had the same idea in mind in getting people baptized in the Jordan River. They want to know how He can justify His actions.

Jesus picks up the veiled allusion to John, and throws it back at them, "When John baptized, did he do it on his own initiative or did he claim to be acting as God's messenger?" If they say that John was right to baptize since he was a prophet, Jesus will then remind them that, as a true prophet, John foretold the coming of a greater one (Mark 1:8), and that will really have the Pharisees backed into a corner.

They maintain a discreet silence, which is the only way they can evade or avoid Jesus' logical thrust. To men who will not commit themselves, Jesus will not commit Himself. For all such discussions are intended to be serious, not word games, not spinning wheels.

Jesus Tells of the Owner's Son/12:1–12

But He does give His answer, although it is couched in the form of a parable. Jesus tells a story, partly to take up the challenge thrown down by the question, "By what authority are you claiming to be the bearer of the Spirit, i.e., the Messiah?" (11:28).

This story of the Owner's Son, as A.M. Hunter calls it,[6] focuses on the person whom the vineyard owner sends "last of all" (12:6). The rebellious tenants hatch a murderous plot (v. 7) whose plan is based on the Jewish law that, if a property stands without an owner or tenant, the people who arrive first on the scene can occupy it and claim "squatters' rights."

They imagine that if they reject the owner's delegates one after another, and then as a crowning defiance, put to death the owner's son, then the property will be theirs since it will be without a legal owner. Conveniently they forget that the owner in a far away country (12:1) still is very much alive and well, even if he lives in absentia. The next stage is for him to get the tragic news of the son's death—and dispatch a punitive mission to give those rebellious tenants what-for (v. 9).

Jesus is here both giving a commentary on current history and making a prediction. He is the Owner's "son and heir"; Israel is the vineyard, and God is the landlord, as Isaiah had said (Isa. 5:1-7). When the rebellious leaders of Israel have killed Him, they will bring down the judgment of God upon themselves, as they did 40 years later when the Romans destroyed Jerusalem and put an end to Jewish hopes of regaining their freedom. But neither Jews nor Romans could destroy Jesus. The building block that the construction crew refused to use becomes, to their utter amazement, the keystone of the arch that holds the edifice in place:

The stone the builders cast aside
Is now the building's strength and pride
(*Psalm 118:22, Moffatt*).

After rejection comes vindication; after Good Friday is the glory of Easter day. This is possible because Jesus is none other than God's Son, declared to be so with power by the resurrection from the dead (Rom. 1:3,4).

It is Jesus' unique relationship to God that gives His rejection by God's other son, Israel (Exod. 4:22), its touching poignancy and pathos. What the privileged Jews failed to see—who Jesus is—is finally grasped by a pagan Roman soldier (Mark 15:39). This is Mark's leading theme which has two sides to it:

1. The Jews are obtuse and at daggers drawn, as verse 8 painfully reports their actions, in staccato tones, "They took him, and killed him, and threw him out of the vineyard" (*RSV*). The other Gospels put the emphasis elsewhere (Matt. 21:39; Luke 20:15) by making the "throwing out" prior to the killing of Jesus. Mark wants to stress the final indignity that He should be killed in the very place—the holy city—where He should have been received and

103

honored. And they intended to leave His body without a decent burial.

2. Then the Gentile centurion is the first to glimpse Jesus' true person, as he stands before the cross (15:39).

Jesus Answers About Taxes/12:13–17

The tribute money incident shows that the Pharisees were continuing to be hostile to Jesus, and to trap Him in debate. Their subtle, trick question, in verse 14, looks easy but it is loaded. It was an issue in which any answer seemed to be incriminating. "Shall we give the poll-tax to Caesar or not? Are we to give it or to withhold it?"

For Him to have said "Yes, pay the tax to Caesar" would be heard as an acceptance of the legitimacy of Roman authority. This would align Him with the (despised) Herodian group who wanted to keep things as they were by collaborating with Rome. To say "No, refuse to pay the tax" would have the effect of countenancing violent revolt and promoting the Zealot cause.

Jesus refused to be impaled on the horns of a false dilemma. The issue is not one of giving voluntarily to Caesar, but paying what is due (v. 17). The Jews enjoy Caesar's government, even if they did not choose to live under it. It gave them good social order, economic stability (even if the sales and food taxes ran high) and worldwide peace, the *pax romana*. These things have to be paid for, as the Pharisees acknowledge by their possession of coins with Caesar's bust and inscription on them (v. 16).

They admit to this possession of Caesar's currency, so let them pay taxes in that coin—and not forget that God is the great benefactor who seeks their willing submission. But there is no inconsistency between political obligation and religious allegiance (as Paul taught also in Rom. 13:1–7).[7]

Jesus Takes the Sadducees to Task/12:18–27

Still smarting from being labeled keepers of a "den of robbers" (11:17) the Sadducees mount a counterattack. These leaders of Israel accepted only the five books of Moses as binding in matters of their faith and practice. In that part of the Bible they professed to find nothing about the afterlife.

The Sadducees' denial of the resurrection (referred to also in Acts 23:7,8) was a bone of contention between them and the Pharisees, who made the resurrection of the dead a central article of their belief. One of the Pharisee documents comes out boldly against the Sadducees: "Whoever says that the resurrection of the dead cannot be deduced from the Torah (the books of Moses) has no part in the Age to Come" (the Mishnah, Sanhedrin 10.1). Jesus was much closer in belief to the Pharisees than to the Sadducees, and the same goes for Paul who was a converted Pharisee (Acts 23:6; Phil. 3:5).

So, to pour scorn on Jesus' teaching, the Sadducees invented an incredible tale of a woman who consecutively was married to seven brothers in one family. "In the resurrection"—which they denied—"whose wife will she be?"(v. 23, *RSV*). They all had married her. Can she in the next world be portioned out to the seven men?[8]

Jesus is a match for them. He doesn't dismiss their story as fantastic. Instead He meets them on their ground, and He bases His reply on a text from the part of the Bible they accepted. In Exodus 3 God announces Himself to Moses as the God of the patriarchs who lived and died years before. But He speaks in the present tense, "I *am* the God of Abraham," etc. So these patriarchs are not really dead and forgotten; they are alive in God. God keeps them alive in His presence, and so there is a hope of eternal life even in the Pentateuch, the book of Moses.

But the Sadducees were ignoring what that life meant. It is not simply an extension or prolongation of this life in another world. It is a new quality of existence where earthly ties are different from what we know now. And it is real life, deeper and richer than we have ever known.

The Sadducees were worldly-minded, money-loving, ambition-seeking, as well as poor, ill-equipped Bible students. This would be bad news for them on the double grounds that (1) their claim to be leaders of Israel was shown to be shaky and (2) their hopes to amass prestige and fortune in this world and let the next world take care of itself were proved to be an illusion, since (said Jesus) death is not the end of the story for anybody.

Perhaps a modern summary of Jesus' response would be: "This is the reason for your terrible mistake. You don't know the Bible or the Prayer book!"[9] He has attacked the Sadducees at their vulnerable flank. And they hated Him for it.

Jesus Asks the Most Important Question/12:28–37

Finally after a day of questions comes the question of the day (12:35–37). There were other matters, all-important, such as the tribute money (12:13–17), and the real meaning of what the law requires (12:28–34) that set Jesus and the Jewish leaders in direct opposition to each other. But nothing comes near to this section where He thrusts the issue of His identity before their eyes in its intrinsic worth. It has been the central question of Christianity ever since.

"What think ye of Christ?" is the test
To try both your state and your scheme.
You cannot be right in the rest,
Unless you think rightly of Him.
                                                    John Newton

Popular expectation was geared to the hope of a forth-coming leader as "Son of David." This hope goes back to 2 Samuel 7:11–16; it is developed in such texts as the prophets' oracles of Isaiah 9:2–7; 11:1–9; Jeremiah 23:5,6, 30:9; Ezekiel 34:23,24; 37:24, and it plays a central role in the expectations at Qumran and the pre-Christian *Psalms of Solomon* which has the line: "Look, O Lord, and raise up for them their king, the Son of David." In all of this hope the Messiah is pictured as a political, earthly figure.

The point of the dialogue in this section is: How can David's Son, the Messiah, be both a descendant of David (and so inferior to him) and one to whom David looks up and calls Lord? Jesus poses it to the embarrassment now of His critics. They have no answer, because they will persist in believing that the expected deliverer is just a political figure. Jesus, in effect, denies this. True, He comes as a loyal son of Israel, born of David's family. But He is no worldly liberator (as the Zealots wanted), nor a supporter of the *status quo* (as the Sadducees hoped for), nor a religious teacher the Pharisees could manipulate and use.

As the true Messiah, He "does not simply extend the work of David, but comes to establish a wholly different Kingdom, the throne of which is situated at God's right hand. . . ."[10]

The Kingdom of God is not territorial and political, but realistically spiritual as God's rule over human lives in society. Jesus is much more than earthly Messiah; He is divine Lord who fulfills Psalm 110:1 at the resurrection and exaltation (Rom. 1:3,4; Phil. 2:9–11; 2 Tim. 2:8).

Jesus is "the Man who fits no formula," as E. Schweizer has recently called Him.[11] That's because He is David's Lord, and God's only Son.

Jesus Notices the Widow's Two Coins/12:41–44

Once more we see Mark's craftsmanship as he draws our attention away from the religious leaders—the Pharisees and Sadducees with their loaded questions and their blatant challenges. Jesus sits quietly opposite the Temple treasury watching people putting in their money (12:41–44). Many rich people give. One poor widow drops in two coins. It is all she has. It is true giving. Of such is the Kingdom of God.

WHAT DOES IT MEAN TODAY?

"They came to Jerusalem" (11:15, *RSV*). So the climax of Jesus' ministry is achieved as He and His followers set foot within the gates of Israel's holy city. Something of the pilgrim's longing to be found in the city of God is given in Psalm 122, which is full of this intensely patriotic and fervent desire to worship the Lord in His house in Zion, the city of David.

Public worship of God in the company of His people is a matter of concern to us all, if we want to follow our Lord's example both in these chapters and throughout His earthly life (Luke 4:16: "as His custom was, He went into the synagogue on the Sabbath day." Contrast Hebrews 10:25

as a warning against some early Christians who were "abandoning the church," as their custom was). How can we overhaul and improve our attitudes to worship in the light of what we have just been studying? Here are some suggestions:

1. "My house shall be called a house of prayer for all nations. You have made it a robbers' den" (11:17). Mixed together, in the Temple forecourt, were religious practices and commercial interests in an unholy rivalry and a fierce competition. Imagine the scene: Gentiles trying to pray in a spot reserved for them, while all around them were bleating sheep, fluttering doves in crates, snorting animals—all waiting to be sold for sacrifice and the constant clink-clink of counting the shekels. How could anyone ever concentrate on God and eternal issues, with the traffic of the world swirling around His feet?

How can we today ever really get through to God if our minds are full of Monday morning's business deals or Saturday's tennis game or the Sunday brunch where the socializing housewife can shine among her peers? Worship involves *concentration*, and an attitude of detachment from earth's ties so that we can "behold the beauty of the Lord, and . . . inquire in His temple." (Ps. 27:4, *RSV*). But one sure way to miss this encounter is to allow one's thoughts to be absorbed with the world's concerns; good and right in their places but a distraction to worship "in spirit and in truth." And there is always the danger of letting these matters dominate and destroy the spirit of communion with God, as Amos 8:5,6 clearly and caustically remarks.

2. "When you stand praying forgive whatever you have against anyone, in order that your Father who is in heaven may also forgive you your offenses" (11:25). We all know what this verse means, and how deadly destructive an uncharitable spirit can be. Jesus' words really hit home on target: How dare we ask to be forgiven by God if we cherish mean thoughts, harsh criticisms and an unforgiving intolerance of other people? We cut ourselves off at one stroke from real fellowship with the Lord and other Christians by

such hypocrisy and divisive, two-faced attitudes.

So, all worship begins with a contemplation of the holy Lord, and that act issues in a cry of penitence and confession, "God be merciful to me a sinner . . . O Lord, pardon my sin, and create in me a clean heart."

We show the sincerity of that petition by declaring in our hearts that we forgive our neighbor who has wronged us; we apologize for our lack of love and concern for that person; and we reach out to touch him or her with compassion and help. Only at that level is our prayer to God to be forgiven worthwhile. *On any other basis the prayer is an unholy sham and a perverse caricature,* which deserves not to be heard. And Jesus emphatically stated (11:26), it will never be heard!

3. The Jewish leader who came with a sincere, well-meaning question (12:28–34) was welcomed for what he was: open, honest, perceptive, insightful. Jesus all but commended him. Yet he had a fatal flaw: "You are not far from the kingdom of God" (v. 34, *RSV*). "Not far," so near, but not yet there. He had run 1,755 yards in a mile race, but he didn't finish the course because he came short in one decisive matter. What was it?

We can only guess, since the Scripture is tantalizing in what it doesn't say. My view is that here was a man who agreed with Jesus 100 percent—in the mind. He approved mentally and enthusiastically all of Jesus' teaching about the commandments. But there it stopped.

He was a hearer of the word, not a doer. Nothing is so frustrating as that. To be in church regularly, to contribute generously, to sing heartily, to applaud choir and sermon warmly, to shake hands vigorously—*but to leave church unchanged.* Two Bible writers force us to look at this matter head-on:

Ezekiel was a powerful preacher, but did he move people to action? (See Ezek. 33:30–33.)

James asks, "What's the use of standing before the mirror and then forgetting to do something about a dirty face or a blemished skin?" (Jas. 1:22–27).

What is true religion? It is faith that works.

Footnotes

1. See Ralph P. Martin, *Mark: Evangelist and Theologian*, pp. 224, 225, and J. Jeremias, *Jesus' Promise to the Nations*, pp. 65f.
2. *The Founder of Christianity*, p. 147.
3. Cited by William Lane, *Commentary*, p. 400.
4. See Ralph P. Martin, *New Testament Foundations*, Vol. 1, pp. 192–3.
5. See Ralph P. Martin, *Mark: Evangelist and Theologian*, p. 201.
6. For the parable of the Owner's Son, see A.M. Hunter, *The Parables Then and Now*, p. 104.
7. On the more controversial question as to whether Jesus accepted a Zealot portfolio of revolution or had any sympathy with nationalism in His day, see Ralph P. Martin, *New Testament Foundations*, Vol. 1, pp. 91–97, with reference to S.G.F. Brandon's thesis and O. Cullmann, *Jesus and the Revolutionaries*, who rebuts it.
8. A story in the apocryphal book of Tobit (chap. 3), printed in the *New English Bible* and the *Jerusalem Bible*, speaks of a woman, Sarah, who had been bereaved of seven bridegrooms as a result of demonic activity. The Sadducees may well have employed this popular tale, since they disbelieved in both the resurrection and demons.
9. The reference to the "power of God" in v. 24 may just possibly refer to a section of the Jewish prayer book used in the synagogue, which is called "the Power." In the same prayer book God's power is praised as that which raises the dead.
10. William L. Lane, *Commentary*, p. 438.
11. In his book, *Jesus*, chapter 2.

10
A Look Ahead
Mark 13:1-37

WHERE ARE WE GOING?

A sure sign of advancing old-age is the loss of clear, sharp 20-20 vision that most people suffer as they get on in years. Modern science has come to their aid with the invention of bifocal lenses which enable them to adjust their vision effortlessly by simply learning to direct their eyesight to a lower portion of the lens of their glasses (for close reading) or an upper portion of the lens (for long distances). Now come trifocal lenses for even better adjustments, covering near, middle, and far distances. And that's exactly what we need to wear, figuratively speaking, when we come to look at Mark 13.

We may expect a part of the chapter to deal with Jesus' immediate situation and the experience of the apostolic church (vv. 5–13), a part to be concerned with the Fall of Jerusalem in A.D. 70 preceded by the Jewish War of A.D. 66 (vv. 14–23), and a part of the chapter to show the long distance focus that extends to the end of the age (vv. 24–27). Then, we switch back to earlier periods and closer scenes in verses 28–31, with the last section (vv. 32–37) covering both the time in the unknown future (at v. 32) and a situation that calls for the disciples' continual alertness (vv. 33–37).

This oscillation, shifting back and forth, is a bit confusing, but if we keep readjusting our focus the separate parts of the passage do make sense. Let's take a look at them one by one.

WHAT DOES IT SAY?
The Disciples' Questions/13:1–4

Jesus had already hinted that the national rejection of His ministry would have dire consequences for Israel (11: 14; 12:9); then He took up His place by the Temple treasury to observe the people bringing their gifts (12:41–44) for the maintenance of Israel's central sanctuary in Jerusalem. It seems natural that He should be invited to comment on the fate of the holy city.

The four disciples are justifiably proud of this national shrine, which was then nearing its final completion. It was part of King Herod's earlier policy to beautify and enrich God's house as a wonder for all the world to see.

The rabbis comment, with a pardonable exaggeration, that a person who has not seen Herod's Temple (begun many years before this incident in the Gospels; see John 2:20) has never seen a beautiful building in his life! Josephus also pays tribute to the way that visitors to Jerusalem were impressed by the first glimpse they had of the Temple site.[1]

Jesus' reply must have been a heavy blow to the disciples as faithful Jews: No stone will remain upon another, once the Romans have carried through their scorched earth policy. (v. 2).

Naturally, if sadly, they wanted to know when it will happen, and if there are to be signs that the fateful event is on the horizon (v. 4).

The setting for Jesus' answer to this question was the Mount of Olives. And a fitting setting it was. The Mount of Olives was the well-known place of divine revelation in Jewish expectation, as expressed in Zechariah 14. The chosen "inner group" of the four disciples pose two questions

112

that we should try to keep separate in this chapter: (1) When will the fateful destruction of Jerusalem occur? and (2) What has this predicted event to say to the larger issue of the end of the age? The second part of the double-barreled question is based on Daniel 12:7: "When the shattering of the power of the holy people comes to an end all these things would be accomplished" *(RSV)*. Note the similarity of the closing words with the disciples' question in Mark 13:4.

Mention of the book of Daniel is a reminder that chapter 13 of Mark is couched in a form of language and style called *apocalyptic*. That word means a descriptive type of writing, combining elements of symbolism and otherworldly features, by which the end of the age is depicted, but with reference to this world. That observation should put us on our guard against an excessive and distorted literalism in interpreting Jesus' prophecies, while, at the same time, we remember that He is talking about real events in the world's history, past and future.

Furthermore, if the apocalyptic parts of the Old Testament, especially Daniel, give the clue to an appreciation of the Lord's discourse, we should equally well have in mind what the chief purpose of all such speaking and writing was. It was *not* to give secret knowledge to feed the fires of speculation and idle curiosity nor was it a kind of religious hobby to amuse and entertain the reader. The purpose was serious and practical; *it was to encourage the faithful to endure in the hope that God's purposes would surely prevail and His rule be vindicated on earth.* But true hopes need to be distinguished from false notions and bogus promises. So the apocalyptic writings are full of warnings to put God's people on their mettle: "Take heed that no one leads you astray."

As in the parables chapter of Mark 4, the evangelist may have put together into a convenient compendium an assortment of Jesus' prophetic sayings addressed to different themes. This suggestion makes important the need for trifocal lenses today as we take a close look at the verses before us.

The First Scene—
The Experience of the Apostolic Church/13:5-13

The long speech Jesus utters here is His response to the disciples' request, although it includes more than they anticipated.

Let the disciples not jump to hasty conclusions, He says, forewarning them that soon after His leaving them, they would be in danger of being led astray. Bogus prophets will appear, proclaiming the end of the world. They will boast "I am he," and thus laying claim to represent God who alone is the I AM (Exod. 3:14, Isa. 41:4, 47:10). This did happen in later Jewish history as messianic claims were attributed to Simon bar-Kochba at the time of the second Jewish War (A.D. 132–135).

He then tells them there will be terrible happenings, such as wars, earthquakes, and famines. "Wars and rumors of wars," strife among the nations (as in Isa. 19:2), earthquakes and famines are all unhappily part of the ravages wrought on human society by nature's disturbance (Rom. 8:22) and man's sin. All "these things," said Jesus, "are bound to happen" (Mark 13:7) because God is a God whose judgments are in all the earth, and "the history of the world is the judgment of the world."[2]

And they are "the beginning of woes" (v. 8). That is a technical expression to describe the intensified afflictions of God's people seen as a prelude to the deliverance Messiah will bring.

These phenomena happen all the time, and they are no indication that the end is near. Such tribulation entails the suffering of loyal believers, and this would have special relevance for Mark's readers who were tasting the bitterness of Roman persecution, though no doubt a future generation of persecuted believers is also intended.

Verse 9 is an encouragement to stand firm, especially when Christians are arraigned before both Jewish courts ("Sanhedrin and synagogues") and Roman magistrates and emperors ("governors and kings"). Their presence will be a Christian witness *against* the worldly powers that will issue in their judgment by God. This is the sense of the

114

Greek in verse 9, rendered in English versions "a testimony to them."

The good news must be proclaimed in all the world prior to the end. So this limitation means that when phony prophets proclaim that the end of the age is around the corner, they are not to be trusted. There must first be, said Jesus, a worldwide missionary campaign. (v. 10).

Jesus' claim will divide families and households (vv. 12, 13), echoing Micah 7:2–6. The point to observe is the reason why Christians will have to accept misunderstanding, loss and even hatred on the part of their kinsfolk: It is because of their first loyalty to Jesus Christ Himself (v. 13), just as He had to endure the hostility of His own people (Mark 3:21, 31–35).

The Twelve are called to be courageous when they face a hostile world. As they go out to be His missionaries, they must expect hardship and physical suffering. But they have a "secret weapon" in their defense and hidden resources on which they can draw (v. 11). The promise of God's help by the Holy Spirit stands, and the earnest Christian, like the overcomer in Revelation 2:3, will be saved in the end.

The Second Scene—
The Destruction of Jerusalem/13:14–23

The angle of Jesus' vision changes, and He looks ahead to the events leading up to A.D. 70. He describes "the desolating [or appalling] sacrilege" (*RSV*) or "abomination of desolation" (v. 14, *KJV*). This phrase goes back to Daniel 9:27; 11:31; 12:11, where it speaks of an act of desecration that renders the Temple defiled and causes God's saints to be horror-struck. At the time of the Syrian invasion of Palestine in 168 B.C. the pagan ruler Antiochus Epiphanes (so-called the illustrious one) committed such a trespass. He entered the Jerusalem sanctuary and desecrated it by sacrificing to the Greek god Zeus and offering a pig on Yahweh's altar. The book of First Maccabees tells this story, and uses the identical expression: "They erected a desolating sacrilege upon the altar of burnt offering" (1 Macc. 1:54). Subsequently, after the successful Maccabean

115

uprising, this defilement was removed and the Temple sanitized (1 Macc. 4:36–54).

There is a nice problem in the Greek of verse 14: "abomination" is neuter gender, but "where *he* ought not" is masculine. There may be no real significance in this conflict of genders, but it is possible that a personal presence of evil, past or future, is intended.

There are several possibilities as to what the "desecrating sacrilege" has in view historically after the time of Christ. Possibly the reference is to the attempt made by the mad Roman emperor Caligula to set up his statue in the Temple in A.D. 40.[3]

Or it could be a reference to events related to the stress of Jerusalem under siege, such as the mock investiture of the clown Phanni as high priest (according to Josephus) and the horseplay associated with this as he was installed into the sacred office. Alternatively, the bringing in of Roman army standards into the Temple precincts at the victorious conclusion of the war also fits the description in Mark 13:14 of the sacrilege that horrified the defeated Jewish Christians or Jews.

Finally, the term could refer to some future antichrist (an idea sometimes associated with 2 Thess. 2:3,4).

"Let him who reads" (Mark 13:14)—probably refers to the verses in Daniel which describe the desolating sacrilege. This aside is added as an editorial comment in keeping with the general purpose of Mark's recording, which is to exhort the church to steadfastness under trial.

Historically the setting of verses 15–23 is the series of events that immediately preceded the outbreak of the Jewish War in A.D. 66.[4] Within the lifetime of these men (13:30, a "generation" would cover the 40 years from A.D. 30 to A.D. 70), the catastrophic events of the Jewish revolutionary war of independence, begun in A.D. 66, would result in the encirclement of Jerusalem by the Roman general Vespasian, his siege of the city, and its capture under his son Titus in A.D. 70.

Josephus, the Jewish historian, tells the sorry story of these tragic years, and it turned out exactly as Jesus here predicted. For Jewish Christians there was one ray of hope. They received a message by a prophet (sometimes thought to be based on Mark 13:14) that they should quit Jerusalem and go to live in Pella, a town in Transjordan.[5] In this way they escaped the fury of the war and the siege of Jerusalem by the Romans.

But for many Jews there was no way out. The Zealots' last stand at the Masada fort in the desert carved a name of Jewish heroism and patriotism that the modern Israeli state is proud to cherish. Nevertheless, at the time it happened, that last stand was a national disaster.

The abbreviating of days of stress and suffering "for the sake of the elect" (vv. 19,20, *RSV*) is an idea not found in the Jewish literature either of the Old Testament or the intertestamental period (with a single, isolated verse as an exception). Probably, however, the thought of God's mercy in sparing humanity because of His people goes back to Genesis 18 (Abraham's intercession for the cities of the plain) and to Daniel 12:1, which is almost certainly the basis for verse 19 in our passage. Daniel 12:1 describes a time of universal and unparalleled trouble, but the promise is given that "your people shall be delivered" (*RSV*) out of it.

Bogus messiahs and false prophets (13:21,22) had already been predicted in Deuteronomy 13, and their facility in performing impressive "signs and wonders" is no guarantee of their genuineness or their authority from God. Indeed, any such ability is more likely to be demonic in origin, like the false prophecy of Revelation 13:13,14 (cf. 2 Thess. 2:9 which speaks of antichrist's "pretended signs and wonders," *RSV*).[6]

The Distant Horizon—
The End of the Age/13:24–27

It is possible that Jesus is still, in the section of verses 24–27, referring to Jerusalem's destruction, but there are some big problems. For example, what of the cosmic upheavals and how did the Son of man come in power and glory? So it is better to see in 13:24–27 a prophecy that reaches out into the future, and predicts the end-time.

The rationale for placing it here ties in with Jesus' warning of the onset of false Christs and deceiving signs (v. 22). In contrast to their false claims, He will tell of the coming of the true Messiah and the valid tokens of His appearing.

The chief difficulty in this passage is to know how to understand the cosmic upheaval of verses 24,25 as a prelude to the coming of the Son of man "with the clouds" (which is better than "*on* the clouds").

"Clouds" are an Old Testament metaphor for the divine presence in glory, so we *could* interpret Jesus' application of Daniel 7:13 to Himself (v. 26) as applying to His vindication and exaltation (seen in Acts 1:9–11) or to His final *parousia*, His coming from God in glory.[7]

The more usual view sees the cosmic signs, whether literal or figurative (as in Isa. 13:10; 34:4), as altogether future and as heralding the last days of world history. The coming of the Son of man is a movement from heaven to earth, and the accompaniment of the final victory is the "rapture" of the church (as in 1 Thess. 4:15–17).

Notice what this section, which looks to be an independent oracle not addressed to the Twelve or the four disciples, does *not* say: no hint of a millennium, no reference to how He will come in His glory, and no promise to Israel as a special nation. These *may* be part of a prophetic program, but they are not mentioned here. Instead, the emphasis falls on the central issue: When all seems lost and the nations (symbolized maybe in the heavenly orders, referred to as such in verses 24,25, as in Isa. 24:21–23, etc.) are in turmoil, then the Son of man will appear to rescue and reward His Church.

The meaning of "this generation" (13:30), which shall not pass away (from the earth) until all these things take place depends on the choice we make in locating what time is mentioned in verse 26. When does the Son of man come in power and glory? At His ascension and Pentecost, or at the last day?

If the reference is to the enthronement of the risen Lord, obviously the sense of "generation" is precise and literal.

118

Within the lifetime of all His hearers, both hostile and friendly, Jesus' promises were made good, and the Jewish Council "saw" Him seated at the Father's right hand, having reached His throne by an act of God's vindication ("the clouds of heaven," in Mark 14:62).

Alternatively, the prediction of verse 30 can be stretched to reach out to the final days. Then "generation" is just possibly an allusion to the literal generation that survived 40 years to the fall of Jerusalem in A.D. 70, and what they experienced *then* was a foretaste of, or prelude to, the final coming of the Son of man. Or else "generation" means something like "race" (the human race which will still be on earth at the last day) or "Jewish people" who will not be allowed to perish from history until their final destiny is attained.[8]

An intermediate view sees "all these things" as referring back primarily to the events of A.D. 66–70, and interprets Jesus' words of assurance that Jerusalem will fall within the lifetime of His hearers as the only view that makes adequate sense. So, "before the passing of a generation, Jerusalem and the Temple will lie in ruins."[9]

Any interpretation of verse 30 has its unresolved problems. If it speaks primarily to the immediate situation of the disciples and the "generation" of A.D. 30–70, what can we make of this verse that seems to have the final day in its sights? Perhaps here again we need to be mentally agile to switch from the nearer view to the far-ranging vision.

The Distant Scene Is Hidden from All Inquirers 13:28–37

Not even our Lord knows when the end will be, as He says in reverting to the disciples' question in verse 4. He saw clearly the middle vision—the Fall of Jerusalem, but He could give no clue as to the end-time. That secret is locked in the Father's counsels. Why are Jesus' followers not content to leave it there (Acts 1:6)?

Instead of prying into the future, let them get busy with what God does place into their hands (Acts 1:7,8): witnessing and watching.

119

The exquisitely told "parable of the porter" (13:33–37), or doorman, enforces the same lesson as Jesus intended throughout. His pastoral call is "Watch" (v. 37)—be ready and on your toes, whenever the rap is heard on the door (see Matt. 25:1–13). The returning Christ comes as a bridegroom, or like a thief in the night (1 Thess. 5:2; Rev. 16:15). Let the hearers be alert and ready to greet Him.

Watching does not mean that people are so engrossed with the hope of the day of His coming that they can afford to sit back and wait for it with folded arms and idle curiosity, as the Thessalonians were guilty of doing (2 Thess. 2:1,2; 3:6–13). Rather the call to watchfulness is a summons to spiritual alertness and preparedness, like the doorkeeper who knows that his absent master will one day come back. He doesn't know when, but whenever he does return, the household affairs will be in good order. The doorporter doesn't spend all his time looking into the future, but he does accept responsibility so that the returning master will find everything as it should be on his arrival home.

So, "What I say to you I say to all: Watch" (v. 37, *RSV*). Whether His coming is soon or far off, let the disciples prepare themselves now to be ready to greet Him then (1 John 2:28).

WHAT DOES IT MEAN TODAY?

Chapter 13 is a nest of controversy, and is full of thorny problems of Bible interpretation, especially to do with prophecy and the future. "No one will deny," writes Vincent Taylor, "that Mark 13 presents one of the unsolved problems of New Testament exegesis."[10]

Yet we should recall and keep in mind what was said earlier about the purpose of such writings in Scripture. They are there not to tease the mind or titillate the imagination or excite the curiosity, but *to strengthen faith when it is tested.* With that observation to guide and inform us, let's put a few questions to the chapter as a whole, whatever the problematical details may be.

1. "The end is not yet" (v. 7). . . . "False prophets will arise . . . to lead astray, if possible, the elect" (v. 22, *RSV*).

There is always the danger that Christians should be conned into thinking that the end of the world is tomorrow and that the latest happenings to hit the headlines are a sure sign of the Lord's return. We know what havoc this mentality caused at Thessalonica (2 Thess. 2:1,2; 3:11,12), and Paul who firmly believed that Jesus would return in glory is quick to dispel such false notions of sign-seeking and to defuse an unhealthy, all-absorbing concentration on the end of the world. For Paul true convictions about the *parousia* of the Son of man express themselves in patient waiting and earnest endeavor to spread the gospel by faithful living in readiness for that day.

2. Having said that, we should not be guilty of the opposite extreme, which is slackness in service and a failure to heed what the Scriptures point to. The Lord's return will occur when people are least expecting it—witness 1 Thessalonians 5:2,3. But Christians ought to be ready to greet Him whenever He comes. "You are not in darkness" (1 Thess. 5:4), but you should be well-informed, sensitive to what is happening around you in the light of the fulfillments of Bible prophecy, and above all, open to God's grace which has given to the Church the prospect of this "happy hope" in the glorious appearing of Christ the Lord (Titus 2:13). (Read once more Mark 13:33–37.)

3. Which brings us to the great object of our hope, our blessed Lord Himself.

Of all the basic truths which relate to the end of the age, and the fulfillment of prophecy, none can rival this as indisputably the greatest: "The Son of man . . . will come with great power and glory" (13:26).

There are obscure issues and debated texts. But of this central concern in the New Testament there can be no doubt: He will come again—in personal presence (Greek word is *parousia*), in glorious majesty and with the right to rule.

The hope stands secure on a fourfold base:
1. Jesus' own pledged word.
2. The angels' witness as He ascended (Acts 1:11).
3. The apostles' preaching and teaching.

121

4. The Church's expectation as expressed in her creeds,
   confessions, hymns and prayers, all of which cry,
   Maranâ thâ, "Come, Our Lord!" (1 Cor. 16:22).
   Even come, Lord Jesus! Amen.

Footnotes

1. *Jewish War,* V, V, 6.
2. Friedrich von Schiller.
3. *Jewish War,* II, X, 1.
4. On the causes of this war and its trauma for the Jewish people, see Ralph P. Martin, *New Testament Foundations,* Vol. 1, pp. 68–71.
5. The text of the report (given by the church historian, Eusebius) is printed in Ralph P. Martin, *Mark: Evangelist and Theologian,* pp. 70,71.
6. See Ralph P. Martin, *Mark: Evangelist and Theologian,* p. 172.
7. For those interpreters who wish to see verse 26 as the enthronement of the Son of man and His being welcomed by the Ancient of Days (God) as in Daniel 7:13, verses 24,25 have to be taken in symbolic fashion to denote the new beginning of the world history implied in Christ's ascension and the new age of the Holy Spirit. Peter quotes Joel 2:28–32 in Acts 2:19–21 to the same effect.

Then, the angels' mission in Mark 13:27 could be the outreach of the gospel through-out the present age (as in Rev. 14:6), and the "gathering of the elect" could be understood as the building up of a worldwide church. There is a similar picture of gospel history from Pentecost to the parousia given in 1 Timothy 3:16, even if the final parousia is not in view in these texts.

8. See A.L. Moore, *The Parousia in the New Testament,* pp. 131–133.
9. William L. Lane, *Commentary,* p. 478.
10. Vincent Taylor, in *Expository Times,* 60, 1949, p. 94.

11
The Upper Room and the Garden

Mark 14:1-72

WHERE ARE WE GOING?

"The passion is the supreme act of the Messiah, and conversely the Messiahship of Jesus is the explanation of the passion." So wrote R.H. Lightfoot in an accurate summing-up of the final chapters of Mark's Gospel.[1]

The story that began in Galilee is moving inexorably to its climax, and the reader is now ready to contemplate the final scenes of a drama that has been heading for a showdown.

Jesus entered Jerusalem to the shouts of Hosanna (11:9). These cries were associated with the Feast of Tabernacles which celebrated Israel's patriotic destiny. Doubtless the people were full of great expectation that their deliverance from political oppression was at hand. If so, they were in for a letdown and disappointment. Rather, Jesus saw His destiny in connection with the Passover celebration.

So Mark adds a time-notice as the frontispiece of His Passion narrative (14:1,2). We could put it simply as the combination of the Messiah and the Passover: These are the two leading themes of our chapter. And there are three focal points where the two ideas run together: as He is identified by an unnamed woman anointing Him with oil; as He celebrates the last supper; at Passover as He faces His final trials. Watch for them as we follow the accelerating train of events.

WHAT DOES IT SAY?
A Woman Proclaims Jesus' True Identity/14:3–9

The anointing at Bethany is full of indications that Mark intended his readers to see. The pointers are directed to the momentous proposition that Jesus went to His death as God's chosen Agent, the Messiah of Israel.

A woman (14:3) comes to the meal table and breaks a flask of precious perfume over His head.

This action (v. 3) looks like an act of anointing the Israelite (messianic) king as in 2 Kings 9:1–13 (cf. 1 Sam. 10:1). This is Mark's purpose in highlighting the woman's action. She glimpsed who Jesus was, namely, the true king of Israel, and she provided the consecrating oil.

Some of the bystanders, especially Judas (John 12:4,5), see only a disgraceful waste of a priceless commodity.[2] Once the slim neck of the flask is broken, it can never be mended, and its contents are spilled for good. If it was a family heirloom, and passed down from mother to daughter as a family treasure as some think, its loss would be irreparable. Others who were present doubtless were mystified by the act, and could see no reason why Jesus permitted it, especially when the cost of the perfume might have been used to help the poor. The woman was attacked.

So Jesus comes to her defense (v. 6). He called her sacrifice "a lovely deed," and for one special reason. The woman had taken a jar of expensive aromatic oil and had poured it over His head. She has confessed thereby her faith in Him as God's anointed one by supplying the oil to

124

perform a symbolic action as in the stories of 1 Samuel 16:13; 1 Kings 19:16; 2 Kings 9:3. It was her faith in Him as Messiah that thrilled Him.

At an even deeper level, she has prepared His body for burial after death (v. 8). J. Jeremias provides an insight from Jewish customs which applies here.[3]

The Jewish rabbis made a distinction between a *gift* of love and a *work* of love. She offered her perfume as a gift, and thereby she intended to express her affection for and sympathy with Jesus. For Him it was a deed that fell into the category of "a work of love" which stands higher as a duty performed than a simple emotional display or a generous gift. He saw it (in v. 8) as part of the requirement that His dead body should receive the funeral rites in advance.

Jesus here is looking ahead to His violent death as one "numbered among the criminals" (Isa. 53:12). As such, His body would be left to rot or be cast into a common grave and buried without final ceremonies (Isa. 53:9). But the woman has supplied the anointing or embalming aromatics in advance, and so she would prevent His body from thus receiving the indignity of a burial like a criminal.

This unnamed woman was the first individual to glimpse the person of Jesus as crucified Messiah. By her gracious work she had helped forward God's saving plan, and she had played her part in bringing Him to His appointment with destiny.

We can appreciate now why Jesus said that her action would never be forgotten—a prophecy which on the face of it seems so unlikely, but it is fulfilled today as we read these words in our study.

God's Purpose and Judas/14:10,11

We all serve God's purposes. The important thing is whether we do so after the manner of the woman who gladly and gratefully gave her dearest possession to Him and for Him; or whether we do so like Judas, who sold his soul for base reward, yet whose treachery and greed were somehow caught up into the divine purposes, even though he himself went to a terrible fate (v. 21).

125

Notice how reticent the Scripture is in regard to Judas. The Bible writers neither list him as a terrible man who deserved all that was coming to him, nor do they try to penetrate into his psyche and help us to know what made him tick and tell us why he did what he did.

All clues as to his motivation are veiled—except one. He was consumed with a love for money (v. 11). John 12:6; 13:29 tells us a little more. He was the treasurer of the apostles' group and kept the accounts. He used to pilfer what was entrusted to him, and it looks as though they had caught him more than once (John 12:6 uses a continuous Greek tense of the verb: "he was in the habit of taking the contents of the purse") with his hand in the till. Aside from his covetous streak, we are only guessing when we ask, "Why did Judas betray his Lord?"

We know that Satan egged him on (John 6:70, 13:27), but how he allowed himself to be used in this tragic way is an enigma wrapped in a mystery.[4]

It is more important to learn the lesson: Here was a person so near to Jesus in one sense and yet so far removed from Him in spiritual sensitivity.

Passover and the Last Supper/14:13–16

Another unnamed person, this time a man, plays a fleeting role on the Passion stage. A man carrying a jar of water is the sign that will lead to the place arranged for the supper. That would have been an uncommon sight in Palestine, since this household chore was women's work. Jesus used it in the same way that we today might call attention to a man wearing makeup.

Verse 12 presents a chronological problem. It seems to be at odds with the notice in 14:2, which says that the Jewish leaders wanted to arrest Jesus before the Passover season. Also, it seems to equate the first day of Unleavened Bread with the time when Passover lambs were killed in the Temple.

In fact, the lambs were sacrificed during the daylight hours (2:30 P.M.—6 P.M.) on the Jewish month Nisan 14 and the "first day of Unleavened Bread" began at the end of that time-period, which marked a new day in the Jewish calendar (Nisan 15).[5]

Whatever the specific day, the Upper Room was made ready to celebrate the family Passover, which has a two-way look. The faithful Jews take a long glance back into their past history, and recall how God brought their fathers out of Egypt (Exod. 12; Deut. 16). Then, they peer expectantly into the future and sigh for the promised redemption from their present enemies. The single item that binds together past and future is their special relationship to God as His covenant people.

The "four-action shape" of the last supper service in verse 22 is full of significance, and the same procedure is carried forward into the Church's Lord's Supper communion celebration. (1) He took bread (and then the cup); (2) He said grace, as He blessed God for the gifts of food and drink; (3) He broke the bread; (4) and He distributed the elements. Yet the most meaningful part of Jesus' actions was still to come: "He said." These "interpreting words" give a clue to what the Passover in A.D. 33, shared by Jesus and His disciples, was all about.

It is about a covenant centered in His person, symbolized in the bread He hands to them with the words: "This is my body" (v. 22). Some interpreters see here a parable of Jesus' death by which He offers to the disciples a share in His self-offering on the cross.[6] As they eat the bread, they gain a share in Him and His death on the cross. For the body is Jesus Himself.

The Passover symbolism is very important here too, suggesting that as the "bread" of Deuteronomy 16:3 brought to the minds of faithful Jews the reality of their redemption from Egypt, so Jesus' gift of Himself in His body would offer them, the new Israel, life purchased by His sacrifice. John 6:52–59 brings out the spiritual significance of what the eating entails: It is feeding on Christ by faith.

After explaining the meaning of the bread, He tells them the covenant is sealed with blood, as was the Mosaic compact at Sinai (Exod. 24). But this is no animal blood used to ratify the agreement as when Moses took the sacrificial

127

blood and sprinkled it on the book and the people. "This," says Jesus, "is my blood of the covenant, which is poured out on behalf of many" (v. 24). The reference is to Exodus 24:8, but even more so Jesus is consciously taking the prophecy of Isaiah 53:12 and playing the part of the suffering servant whose sacrifice avails for "the many," i.e., the Gentiles.

Again the Passover setting is significant, as is seen in Paul's words in 1 Corinthians 5:7,8: "Christ our Passover is sacrificed. Let us, then, celebrate the festival." Peter echoes the theme (1 Pet. 1:18,19) and so do many statements of Christian devotion, such as this:

Thou very Paschal Lamb,
Whose blood for us was shed,
Through whom we out of Egypt came,
Thy ransomed people lead.

Verse 25 is a sequel to the familiar words spoken over the bread and the cup, but it has a value all of its own. It represents a vow of abstinence made clear in Luke 22:14–18. This is a feature on which some recent discussion has thrown light. J. Jeremias[7] has shown that Jesus abstained from the cup because He had an indispensable part to play as intercessor for His people. Confronted by the tragic refusal of Israel to heed His call, Jesus takes on Himself the work of advocate. It was written of Isaiah's servant, "[He] made intercession for the transgressors" (Isa. 53:12, *RSV*).

Jesus steps right into the breach, and in refusing the cup which would have identified Him as a loyal son of Israel, He ranges Himself on God's side as Israel's intercessor, pleading with God to spare the people and accept His offering in place of their disobedience and rebellion. Already at the Passover table He anticipates the horror of dereliction on the cross when, as both sin-bearer and penitent, He vicariously stood in the gap and brought God and man together in holy reconciliation.

Finally, the covenant brings the disciples into a new relationship with Him beyond death (v. 25). He says he will greet them again in the new age of His Kingdom soon to be established.

128

Let us recap what the last meal in the Upper Room meant to the disciples: a sacrifice in which they had a share; a covenant making them beneficiaries, though they did not deserve it; and a reunion promised with Jesus face-to-face in a joyous fellowship beyond death. These are the pledges Jesus gave at the last supper. These are the realities that can be ours at the Lord's Supper today, which is a celebration, in company with the living Lord and His people, of all He has accomplished by His messianic death and victory.

Jesus' Warning Is Verified/14:27–31; 66–72

Jesus' warning that His fate is closing in around Him is based on Zechariah 13:7–9. However the dismal scene of betrayal and loss is shot through with rays of hope. "After I have been raised (from death), I will go before you" (literally, "I will lead you forth" as a shepherd does his sheep, as in John 10:4) to Galilee. This is exactly how it turned out, according to Mark 16:7.

Peter's protestations of undying loyalty are matched by Jesus' realistic statements that Peter is no better than the other men. He, too, will fail and fall away "before the cock crows twice" (v. 30). Normally this allusion is taken to be to the rooster's call in the early morning, but since the Roman bugle call to denote the third of the four night watches (midnight to 3 A.M.) is called "cock-crow" (Latin *gallicinium*), it may be that Jesus had that sound in mind. The advantage of this idea is that Roman bugles were heard throughout the city.

The sad denials of Peter (14:66–72) are compounded by their repetition, involving him in a standoff with a female servant of the high priest and a bystander who recognizes that he is a Galilean (by his accent: Matt. 26:73). Peter had put himself on the spot by his entry into the courtyard, in Mark 14:54, which was an act of courage. But courage failed him when the interrogation became pointed.

Jesus Prays in Gethsemane/14:32–42

The Gethsemane trial of Jesus can never be fully known. But we still have to ask questions. Our inquiry centers on

129

the petition that the cup should be removed (v. 36). Because the issue raised in the Gethsemane story is so crucial to an understanding of Mark's Gospel, and Jesus' purpose as Mark tells it, we devote an extended amount of space to it.

It is quite out of harmony with all that Mark has previously shown in the Passion sayings of Jesus, to conclude that now His obedience faltered and He began to doubt His mission. Also, it is not quite satisfactory to interpret the prayer: "Abba, Father, all things are possible to thee; remove this cup from me; yet not what I will, but what thou wilt" (*RSV*) as a final questioning on the part of Jesus as to whether His mission would necessarily entail the suffering which He knew to be preliminary to the coming of God's Kingdom.

"All things are possible to thee" points to His conviction that God's Kingdom will come in God's own way. If His own suffering is to precede the establishing of God's reign, He is prepared for it, though now at the final stage of His destined course to Jerusalem He contemplates "the possibility that the wished-for future, the establishing of the Kingdom of God, might come without the necessity of preliminary suffering."[8]

Even when expressed in this guarded way, this interpretation suggests that at the last Jesus envisaged some other issue to His life and mission than one involving His own sacrifice on the cross.

Another possibility is to be considered. This turns upon the precise meaning to be given to the metaphor of the cup. Usually the metaphor is taken to be one or God's wrath or Jesus' human suffering. It could conceivably be a vivid expression of His experience of satanic temptation. Gethsemane, in this view, is indeed the scene of conflict as Jesus for the final time wrestles with the demonic insinuation that He can tread God's path and still avoid the cross.

Throughout His ministry He has been tempted to fulfill His mission in a way which would have gained Him an immediate and positive response. He could have offered an accrediting sign from heaven (8:11–13); He might have capitalized on His wonderful works and commanded a following among people who were impressed with His supernatural powers. He would have received the plaudits of His own disciples if He had promised them thrones (10:37) and good seats in the spectacle of an imminent kingdom.

Instead, He consistently set His face against these false choices and easy roads to success and acclaim. God's Kingdom must be served in God's way; and in a mystery He knows that this *will* entail His obedience unto death.

Now, within the shadow of the cross, He faces His ultimate trial. The pressure to turn back is at its strongest as the hour of His final obedience comes. He prays that the temptation to be unfaithful to His calling may indeed pass as the cup is removed. His testing is real; and the disciples too are involved (v. 38), for in a real sense they would choose, if they could, an easy road for Him which bypassed the cross (8:32). He must, therefore, overcome in His trial and encourage them not to dissuade Him from His goal any further.

Jesus wins through to a final oblation of His will to God, and in an ultimate submission yielded His life to God as His obedient servant and trustful Son. "Rise, let us be going" (v. 42) is His rousing call, as He marches forward to meet His betrayer, His enemies and His freely embraced fate.

Judas Betrays Jesus/14:43–52

Somewhat out of sequence, but following our plan to track the effects of this night's events on Jesus, we come now to Judas' betrayal. It begins with verse 41: "Are you still asleep? still resting?" Then comes a tantalizing expression whose meaning is uncertain. Notice the wide diversity of possible meanings of the one Greek verb *apechei* (usually translated, "It is enough," in verse 41.)

1. "Is he (Judas) far off?" No! He's here.
2. "Far from it." Get up, the hour has come.
3. "Is the end far away?" No, it's soon.
4. "He has been paid in full," with 30 pieces of silver.
5. "He is coming to take me," referring as in no. 4 to Judas.[9]

131

Judas arrived, and led the armed mob straight to Jesus. But the failure of the remaining 11 men is only a few notches less in its pathos: "They all left him and fled" (v. 50).

One person nearly got caught in the mêlée. Who he was and how he managed to escape will never be known for sure. Some like to think of him as John Mark who wrote the Gospel, while others see here a painful fulfillment of Amos 2:16. His getaway sharply contrasts with the fate of Jesus who refused to escape and allowed Himself to be seized.

Jesus Is Condemned by the Sanhedrin/14:53–65

This section serves one purpose, which is to show how Jesus was condemned by the Jewish court, the Sanhedrin. The proceedings are more like an arraignment than a trial. The object seems to have been to fasten some accusation of indictable offense on Jesus which will make a transfer of His case to the Roman official, Pilate, a necessary next step.

What is given in these verses is best called a preliminary hearing. It was informal and not too careful about strict legal procedures. So it was held at night, contrary to legal requirements for an official trial. But it wasn't such a trial, so this may explain the irregularities.

The same fact answers a pressing question: If the Jewish authorities "tried" Jesus and found Him guilty (as they did, according to verse 64), why did they not proceed, immediately after the sentence had been passed, to carry it out by stoning, the prescribed penalty for blasphemy (the charge in v. 64), according to the law (Lev. 24:10–23)? The answer is that (1) this was *not* a formal capital trial, because (2) the Sanhedrin did not have, at that time, the power to pass sentence of death and carry it out. (So says John 18:31, 32.)[10]

There may be deeper issues involved. G.D. Kilpatrick in his lecture, *The Trial of Jesus,*[11] offered the view that the Sanhedrin inquiry was a ploy by the Sadducees to show that Jesus was a public danger, and to convince the Pharisees that they should join in getting Pilate to act because Jesus was guilty equally of treason against Rome.

Most recently, Judge H.H. Cohn of the Israeli Supreme Court has argued this court was held to save Jesus from the Romans. The intention was to prove Jesus' innocence by gettng Him to plead "not guilty" and to resolve not to break the peace again. The plan broke down because Jesus wouldn't go along with it, and insisted on asserting His messianic claims. So the Jewish council had no choice but to remit the matter to Pilate.

This is an ingenious reconstruction, but the thesis (stated in Cohn's *The Trial and Death of Jesus*)[12] collapses on the unproven notion that the evangelist is anxious to shift the blame for Jesus' death from the Romans to the Jews—an idea shown to be implausible by A.N. Sherwin-White, *Roman Society and Roman Law in the New Testament*.[13]

"The real offence of Jesus lay, not in the fact that He said, 'I am,' but in the fact that He said nothing. Silence was the offence, because it was a contempt of court which made Him, in effect, a rebel against it."[14]

In fact, the claim to be Messiah would not, technically speaking, lead to the charge of blasphemy. What was additionally incriminating was Jesus' insistence that He would overthrow the Temple (so dearly venerated by the Sadducees) and that He would build another Temple, altogether divine ("made without hands").

Jesus, true to His earlier teaching, set greatest store by His self-chosen title, Son of man (v. 62). He predicted that His hearers would live to see the day when the Son of man was exalted with the clouds of heaven. In context, this can only relate to His resurrection, ascension and the installation of Jesus as Lord (fulfilling Ps. 110:1)—the effects of which were seen in the coming of the Holy Spirit at Pentecost and the establishing of the Church.

Jesus Faces His Final Trials—A Summary

"Not without great danger to himself, which made me love him the more," says John Bunyan in an aside, as he comments in *Pilgrim's Progress* on Christian's talk with the

133

three ladies at the House Beautiful and as their conversation turned to the Lord. Exactly what the cost of human salvation meant is partly spelled out in these verses. Our Lord faced trials at different levels.

1. He bore the cowardice of Peter who was so brave before the event (15:27–31), yet turned out to be so miserable a failure when put to the test (vv. 66–72). With loud protests he professed to stay with Jesus to the last. Now he is among the first to disown him as he warms himself at the fire but there is a chill, a streak of fear, running through his soul.

2. The publicity and shame of a trial before the Jewish council (or Sanhedrin) must have struck deep into the loyal heart of Jesus (vv. 53–65). He had to face the trumped-up charges as His words were wrenched from their context and distorted as "evidence" against Him. He suffered the indignity of a question (v. 61) designed simply to incriminate Him before a court of law.

Then came the charge. He is judged guilty of blasphemy (v. 64), and then come the insults and the blows (v. 65).

3. In His mind there would be mingled sorrow and pain over Judas who betrayed Him (vv. 43–49). The enigma of Judas remains as a solemn mystery and a warning to all. Yet we cannot escape the grim irony of the garden treachery. Not with a shout, a blow, or a stab—but with a kiss, the token of love and endearment, the Son of man is delivered to His foes. And Judas goes off to collect his fee for services rendered.

4. We have not yet plumbed the full depths of Jesus' trial. In 14:32–42 we see the heavy weight of personal involvement in His ministry. The place is Gethsemane, the wine-press which He trod alone (Isa. 63:3). The best commentary on this moving scene is Hebrews 5:7,8 which forces upon us the inescapable question: Granted we see Jesus' courage when faced with death's awful prospect, what was it He prayed to have pass from Him (vv. 35,36)? And was His prayer heard and answered, as Hebrews 5:7 suggests that it was?

Dogmatic answers are out of place, but no solution can

satisfy that suggests or even hints that His purpose of obedience faltered or that He backed away from the cross. To this destiny He had come by deliberate choice and long preparation. What He asked to be removed was satanic temptation that insinuated here as before that there was some other way to save the world.

"Remove this cup" (v. 36). So He prayed, and so it was removed by God. Then, with a final resolve to embrace the Father's will, even at unspeakable cost, He goes forth to yield His life to men and their evil designs (vv. 41,42). But through it all, He is committing that life to His Father's design and holy purpose for the salvation of the world—a salvation that can only be achieved by His death.

WHAT DOES IT MEAN TODAY?

This chapter divides into three parts; each part poses its questions and presents its challenges.

1. Here is a woman who has remarkably perceptive insight, understanding, courage to dare, and willingness to go to extreme lengths to demonstrate her love and confess her faith. Is it any wonder Jesus memorialized her in a prophecy that can be shown to be true? Haven't we just proved that she will always be remembered by reading the story once again?

Several features come together in her act. She wanted to give a costly display of love, to the point of sacrifice. She wanted to confess her faith in Jesus as Israel's anointed one. She contributed a share in the ongoing purpose of God by which His Son came to His destiny and to His victory beyond death.

Is there some aspect we can relate to? Is my love for Christ lavish? Is my witness to Him bold? Is my life fitting in to God's plan?

2. Jesus shared the last meal with His friends, and dramatized, in a way that words could never do, the meaning of His death and triumph.

Every Lord's Supper service serves this purpose, with its fourfold direction:

(1) We look back to the Upper Room and the cross, and

gratefully see our finished salvation. The body and the blood are "for us"—once offered, finally given, never to be changed. It's the good news of dying love, free grace, full atonement, and all of this should evoke our "Eucharist," meaning thanksgiving.

(2) We look within, to search our hearts. "Lord, is it I?" each disciple asked, when they might easily have glanced at a neighbor or muttered something under their breath about Judas.

(3) We look upwards, since the crucified is the risen Lord, the Lamb upon His throne (Rev. 5), and present now by the Spirit with us as we are gathered in His name. At the table, there is a "real presence," known to faith and apprehended by love.

(4) We look ahead, as Jesus did (14:25). He anticipates a future reunion, and we'll be there to celebrate with Him, at the final homecoming of God's people in all ages (Rev. 19:6–10).

The earliest Christian prayer was *Maranâ thâ* (1 Cor. 16:22), "Our Lord, come!" It was a request for Him to meet His people at the table, and to appear in final glory.

3. We tread on holy ground when we enter the garden of Gethsemane. If ever the reminder were needed, it is needed here: *The soul of His sufferings were the sufferings of His soul.*

Jesus faced death with resolution and trust, yet He was "in an agony." It was a conflict, not a charade. It was a real struggle, not a piece of play-acting. He was victorious, but only because He was determined to accomplish the Father's purpose and see it through to the end.

Out of this scene we hear His call: "Watch and pray, lest you enter the test" (14:38).

Footnotes

1. R.H. Lightfoot, *History and Interpretation in the Gospels*, p. 141.
2. "Three hundred denarii," the estimated cost of the oil, represent a considerable sum of money, based on Matthew 20:1–16 and Revelation 6:6.

3. *New Testament Theology*, Vol. 1, p. 284.

4. For a brief survey of theories, see *New Bible Dictionary*, pp. 674, 675.

5. The difficulty is perhaps more apparent than real, and there have been some suggestions made to overcome it; see Ralph P. Martin, *New Testament Foundations*, Vol. 1, p. 198.

6. Vincent Taylor, *The Gospel According to St. Mark*, p. 544.

7. *New Testament Theology*, Vol. 1, p. 298.

8. C.K. Barrett, *Jesus and the Gospel Tradition*, pp. 46, 47.

9. See H. Anderson, *The Gospel of Mark*, p. 321.

10. See A.N. Sherwin-White, *Roman Society and Roman Law in the New Testament*, p. 32–47.

11. *The Trial of Jesus.*

12. *The Trial and Death of Jesus.*

13. See H. Anderson, *The Gospel of Mark*, p. 327, for the conclusion that both Romans and Jews were implicated and were in collusion *from the very outset* in the proceedings that culminated in Jesus' death (author's italics).

14. J. Bowker, *Jesus and the Pharisees*, p. 50.

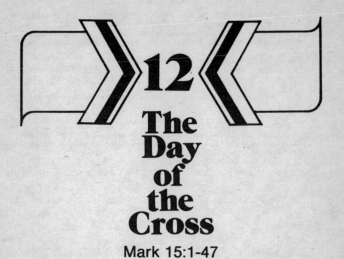

12

The Day of the Cross

Mark 15:1-47

WHERE ARE WE GOING?

Back in the year 1909 W.M. Clow, a notable preacher and minister in Glasgow, Scotland published a volume of sermons entitled *The Day of the Cross.* The central, organizing theme of these pulpit utterances was a study of the men and women who are seen on the stage of the Good Friday drama. But the preacher was too expert an expositor and too sensitive a pastor to miss the real significance of the way the Gospels present the crucifixion of Jesus. So he draws attention repeatedly to what is his main purpose. This is *to see through the personalities of the Passion to the mind of the Lord Himself.*

Modern study of the Gospels has strikingly endorsed this purpose. The men and women who appear on the scene, and even those who have "speaking parts" to play, do so, not for their own sake, but in order to help the reader see more of what the cross meant to Jesus Himself. This is the preeminent principle of Gospel interpretation, and it is the key to an understanding of Mark 15.

The way in which the Gospel records angle the history they record and the story they tell in order to put all of their emphasis on Jesus Himself is such a vital matter that we should pause to elaborate it.

A quick reading of the Good Friday drama might suggest otherwise. We might suppose that it is other people who are wielding the power and tugging at the puppets' strings. Jesus seems to be caught in the vortex of a political struggle of Jews *versus* Romans. He seems caught between the hammer and the rock, and crushed by the blow that falls.

Apparently this is so; but not really. Though He keeps His counsel and seems to be passive in all the events that swirl and eddy around Him, in fact He is still Lord. This is a basic element in the Christian story: *His Passion is action.* He suffers by His own choice and deliberate accepting of the Father's plan. He will yield His life to men, but more, He is doing God's will, though it involves pain and unbelievable loss, even involving the time when the Father's presence is momentarily withdrawn, as He goes out in the aloneness of being forsaken and receiving, in that grim moment, the judgment of God upon sin (15:34).

But He knows what He is doing, though it costs more than we can tell.

Mark's Gospel was most likely written in Rome and for Roman Christians. It cannot therefore be accidental or incidental that three characters who have connections with Rome dominate the scenario of chapter 15. By contrast, Jesus remains strangely silent and submissive. From 14:50 when He is arrested in the Garden, He speaks only three times (14:62, 15:2,34). Repeatedly He maintains a passive silence. We can see this in 15:5 and especially 15:29–32 where, for a final time, the enemies of Jesus taunt Him and invite Him, mockingly, to give a sign. But He is uncooperative with this idea, as before (8:11–13).

So, our conclusion about chapter 15 stands in its stark reality. Jesus is silent. Others do the acting and speaking, and our interest focuses on what they say and do.

Mark's readers would find immense comfort and strength just here: they were experiencing suffering and pain as persecuted Christians *for the first time* when Nero began to punish them with death. No doubt, they too were asking, "My God, why have you forsaken us?" like the martyrs' cry in Revelation 6:9–11. The answer comes back: Be patient and God will bring you through suffering to glory, just as He did the Lord Himself. Also, they would recall the example of Jesus who didn't answer back when He was incriminated, and they would take a lesson in endurance, such as Peter advised in the same historical situation of Nero's persecution of the church. (Read 1 Peter 2:20–23; 3:15–17.)

If we can hold these two ideas in mind, it helps us to understand how the first readers of the Gospel may well have reacted. And that's what Bible study is all about; it's the name of the game.[1]

WHAT DOES IT SAY
The Roman Judge/15:1–20

Before the Jewish council, the charge leveled against Jesus was blasphemy. Now as the case is remitted to the Roman governor, it is high treason against the state. The full statement of the indictment is given in Luke 23:2. Notice that the common element is one of the most damaging of all. Jesus was claiming to be "King of the Jews." The Jewish authorities wouldn't accept that. And to Pilate, the sensitive official who was concerned above all to keep the province of Judea quiet and free from revolutionaries, this title would be like a "red flag to a bull."

Pontius Pilate was the Roman representative whose procuratorial headquarters were in Caesarea on the Mediterranean coast. But he had come to Jerusalem to keep an eye on things at the crowded Jewish Passover festival.

Pilate had already tasted a little of Jewish patriotic sentiment when it was stirred to fierce, nationalistic reaction. He was still smarting under the humiliation he suffered at the hands of the Jewish leaders. They had tried to block his plans to divert money from the Temple treasury to a fund to finance water supplies into Jerusalem. And the result was a riot and much bloodshed.

There was also the recent event of Sejanus' fall from power at Rome. Sejanus had encouraged the emperor Tiberius in the direction of anti-Semitism. Now with Sejanus' downfall, Pilate had lost a patron and an influential supporter, and he was well aware that the emperor was in favor of a pro-Jewish policy. The last thing in the world he wanted was trouble at the Passover of A.D. 33. It was bad news indeed when the Jewish leaders came, early in the morning, with a charge the prefect could not ignore.

So with Pilate in a very delicate position the dialogue began with a cross-examination.

Pilate: "Are you 'the King of the Jews'?"

Jesus: "You do well to ask." (Literally the Greek runs, "You say it," but it is less than a positive yes, since that would have brought the conversation to an abrupt close, the prisoner having admitted a plea of guilty. Jesus deflected Pilate's question, to get him to think what kingship is all about.[2])

More accusations and innuendos tumble out. Pilate is getting short-tempered (v. 4). But Jesus knows that any answer in such an atmosphere, so hostile to Him, will be worse than useless. So He fulfilled Isaiah 53:7, and "he did not open his mouth" (*RSV*).

As the Roman prefect (this is his more accurate title, better than "procurator" or "governor") he was committed to see justice done. Yet he was too sensitive of his own precarious office to want to offend the Jews, and they had brought Jesus to him on a political charge. Or so it seemed. So Pilate tried to get himself off the hook by offering to release Jesus and transfer the blame to a public enemy no. 1, called Barabbas who was awaiting execution on a Roman death-row (15:6–15).

The choice of setting up an option of "Jesus *versus* Barabbas," often called the paschal amnesty, has been called in question as a historical fact.[3] What stands out in the contemporary situation in which Pilate was involved is the fact that the Roman prefect was clearly a man under pressure.[4] This sensitivity to Jewish opinion, lest he himself should fall foul of their evil-minded hostility (referred to in

15:10), accounts for his rather strange, vacillating behavior that historians find to be so unbecoming and erratic in a stern Roman official. In 15:15 Mark puts his finger on the exposed nerve: "Pilate, wishing to please the crowd, released Barabbas to them, and after having Jesus thrashed, he delivered him over to be crucified."

When all else failed, he had no choice but to pass sentence. No choice that is, provided he was prepared to put prestige and rank before conscience and the plain dictates of duty. But that was the price he was willing to pay. What did he get in return? An ambiguous immortality as his name is recited on a million lips who chant the Apostles' Creed every Sunday across 2,000 years: "suffered under Pontius Pilate." He is that Roman governor whose weak will and selfish ambition allowed him to compromise because he wouldn't let go his desire for renown and honor.

The soldiers' horseplay and mockery (15:16–20) is filled out by what we read in John 19:13. The scene is set at the Pavement, probably identified (since Vincent's archaeological work in Jerusalem in 1930) as the mosaic floor in the Antonia fort, which is now near the church of the Sisters of Sion. There the Roman soldiers practiced a mock "carnival," involving the dressing of a prisoner in royal robes and greeting him as though he were Caesar ("Ave Caesar" is the " 'Hail, King of the Jews' " in verse 18).

The "crown of thorns" (v. 17) is a caricature of the crown worn by the emperor as a sign of his claim to divinity. The soldiers pressed it on Jesus' head as a cruel parody and rough joke. But, whatever the intent of the crown of thorns may have been, Christians have always seen in it a token of the crown that Jesus now wears in glory as the "Lamb slain . . . who is on the throne" (Rev. 5:6,12; 19:12).

The Passerby and the Roman Soldier/15:21–37

"They led him out to crucify him" (v. 20, *RSV*). Death by this method of capital punishment was dreaded even in the hardbitten Roman world. It was not a Roman practice originally, but it was introduced from the eastern lands. The Romans practiced it as a salutary warning to rebels and criminals, while at the same time excusing their own citizens from such a terrible and terrifying fate. Writers like Cicero recoil from the thought of the cross and, in one vivid passage, Cicero labels crucifixion as the "most cruel and horrifying punishment" meted out to abject persons.

Contemporary writers have provided some data about the methods employed. We know that the flogging was in itself a frightening, often lethal, prelude. Then, the condemned person had to carry the crossbeam to the place of execution. The notice, called a *titulus*, bore the record of the victim's crimes, referred to in verse 26. All these details are borne out by the narrative in our Bibles.

But, it was in June 1968 that Israeli archaeologists unearthed for the first time a collection of bones which are attributed to Jewish victims who died by Roman crucifixion. The most interesting find was at Giv^cat ha-Mivtar in the northeast section of Jerusalem near Mount Scopus. Examinations of the remains prove that the victim was tortured by being affixed to the cross in an unnatural crosswise position, with knees doubled up and trunk contorted. Found in an ossuary, the bones show clear marks of having been split or fractured by the nails used in crucifixion, and medical science at the Hadassah Medical Center in Jerusalem has been able to reconstruct the way in which victims were impaled.[5]

It is not a pleasant reminder that Jesus suffered before He died, but it is a fact of history.

The first man in the scenario of this passage is Simon (15:21). Though Cyrene in North Africa (Acts 2:10) is given as his place of origin, his home was evidently in Jerusalem or else, more likely, its environs. He had come to the city for the feast. But the interest of Mark's readers would be drawn directly to the names of his sons, Alexander and Rufus. The latter name appears in Paul's letter to the Romans 16:13 where greetings are sent to a certain Rufus, and commentators consider it very possible that this is the man mentioned by Mark. He was a member of the church in Rome.

To Rufus' father, then, we may surmise, fell the honor of

carrying the crosspiece called a *patibulum* that all condemned criminals were forced to bear to the execution.

The Gospel writer Mark records this detail without elaboration, though it must surely have taken the reader's mind back to 8:34: "If any man would come after me, let him deny himself *and take up the cross* and follow me" (*RSV*, italics added). Many in Mark's church were doing what that implied. They were dying for their faith at the time of Nero's persecution against the Church in Rome. They would recall Simon, the father, as a man they knew well, and take courage.

"Golgotha" (15:22) is interpreted as the "place of a skull," a feature drawn from the shape and contour of the hill. Luke 23:33 calls it simply "The Skull," the Latin for which is *Calvaria* or Calvary. The present-day site is either near the Church of the Holy Sepulchre or the so-called Gordon's Calvary, after the man who thought he had identified a round hill near the Garden Tomb.

The "wine spiced with myrrh" (Mark 15:23) was a rude narcotic offered to the victims to help them endure the pain. It was evidently the work of a society of charitable Jewish women who made it their business to perform this service at crucifixions. Jesus tasted the cup, then He refused, since He would not have His senses clouded for the ordeal that awaited Him. He had the work of atonement to accomplish—it was His time for action—and for that He needed all His faculties alert.

The time-notices (15:25,33,34) indicate that Jesus was crucified at 9 A.M.; the darkness came upon the land at noon; and He breathed his final gasp at 3 P.M.

Central to His purpose was Jesus' cry of desolation (15: 34): "My God, my God, why have you abandoned me?" The Gospel writers do not harrow our feelings. Their interest lies in the work of atonement.

This is the most mysterious of the seven words He spoke at Golgotha. This cry of dereliction has to be taken at face value.[6]

Basic to an appreciation of something that is, in reality, beyond our comprehension is the meaning of Deuteronomy 21:23. The person "hanged on a tree" is under God's judgment, a text illuminated by the Dead Sea Scrolls in which Alexander Jannaeus is regarded with contempt because he "hung up men alive" and so brought upon them the curse of the Deuteronomic text. The acceptance by Jesus of this judgment of God is part and parcel of His vocation as Isaiah's suffering servant (Isa. 53:10–22), a destiny He claimed for Himself according to Mark 10:45. In that awful moment, His soul was made "an offering for sin" as the "ransom for many," and He died vicariously to bear the sins of others.

He dies to atone
For sins not His own.

Paul will later make this a pivot in his interpretation of the cross (Gal. 3:13; 2 Cor. 5:21; Rom. 5:10–11). But there is still a mystery in this cry. "God, forsaken by God," asked Luther. "How can it be?" "It was as though God turned atheist," commented Dorothy L. Sayers.

His call to God as Eli, "my God" (from Ps. 22:1) was misheard as an invocation of Eli-jah. But a natural misunderstanding led to a kindly deed (Mark 15:36). An unnamed Roman soldier soaked a sponge in the *posca* which was a mixture of egg, vinegar, and sour wine and was available to soldiers on duty. He placed it on a reed to lift it to His parched lips. It rescues the grim scene of Calvary from unrelieved horror to recall that there was a thoughtful action from an unexpected Roman source.

The Roman Centurion/15:38,39

This man was evidently the officer who was in charge of the execution squad. Throughout the grim ordeal he was impressed by all that had taken place at this strange public execution. The phenomena he couldn't understand included the darkness (v. 33), the demeanor of the crucified and His expiring cry (v. 39), and perhaps the sight of the inscription fixed over His head as the *titulus* which gave the accused man's crimes (v. 26). All of this surely made a vast impresssion on him, and he cries out, "Truly this man was God's Son."

There are several things to observe. Mark has skillfully placed this single verse in close connection with verse 38, which in turn interrupts the flow of the story. The sequence is artistic. First, Jesus' loud cry (probably the one recorded in John 19:30). Then, our attention is switched to the Temple area, and to the Most Holy Place where the separating curtain is torn by an unseen hand, as if to symbolize a breaking down of the barrier that kept men out from God's presence (the curtain referred to in Heb. 10:19-22).

It is uncertain whether Mark intended to refer to the outer curtain, separating the sanctuary from the forecourt, or the inner veil which divided the sanctuary and the Holy of Holies. The first curtain was on public view, and its rending could have been seen by all. The phenomenon is taken by church Fathers, such as Tertullian and Chrysostom, to be a sign of the Temple's fate, thus confirming Jesus' prognostication in 13:2.

But the symbolic meaning, to do with access into God's presence now available through the torn curtain, was probably uppermost in Mark's mind. This would identify the veil with the inner curtain, as in Hebrews 6:19; 9:2f.; 10:19f. The close association of the next verse, relating to the Gentile soldier's confession of faith, argues in favor of the second interpretation.[7]

Finally, we revert to the scene on the hill, and we learn that it is a pagan soldier who first benefits from this new access. He enters the holy place and, with the Christian confession on his lips—the attestation of faith in Jesus as Son of God that runs through Mark's Gospel from the start (1:1) to its conclusion—he becomes the first sign of the great Gentile ingathering from the Roman world. Familiar with the idea that the Roman Caesar is a son of the gods, this man now utters the confession that brought Christians into direct collision with the worship of the emperor. There is no king but Jesus. He alone is God's only Son.

Mark's Gospel reflects the situation of the Church in a hostile world. Therefore, it speaks to our needs today. Like Pilate, we face the subtle temptation to compromise and to silence conscience's insistent voice. Yet we see kindly

146

deeds done that often put us to shame—and that call us to outthink, outlove and outdie the world. The great words on the centurion's lips are a promise of a harvest yet to be reaped and a reminder that we should not despair of God's cause nor doubt the crucified's victory.

Joseph of Arimathea boldly came to Pilate to gain permission to bury Jesus' body (15:23,44). Pilate expresses surprise that He had died so quickly. Victims often lingered for two or three days on the cross.

The reference to Pilate's agreement with the desire to have Jesus interred serves several purposes. It shows that, after all, the Roman prefect recognized that Jesus was no common criminal who received His just deserts. Ordinarily, victims were not buried, but their bodies were left exposed to rot or to be consumed by predatory beasts and birds. More importantly perhaps, it showed that Pilate was satisfied that Jesus had really died. The burial was tantamount to a death certificate. Therefore, if Jesus was known to be alive after Easter day, it must be by a resurrection, since it is clear that He was killed and was buried in a grave. Hence the insertion of the clause "He was buried" in the first Christian creed in 1 Corinthians 15:4 and in the later Apostles' Creed: "crucified, dead, *and buried.*"

WHAT DOES IT MEAN TODAY?

The "story of the cross," declared Paul, is to those of us who are saved the power of God (1 Cor. 1:18). Sadly it is just as true that to an unbelieving world it is a message that is dismissed as foolishness.

Over Jesus' head they placed this wording on a board: "Jesus of Nazareth, the King of the Jews" (John 19:19 gives the full title). This would be in Latin (as well as other languages) for the benefit of the Romans; and it is abbreviated as INRI.

Joe Orton, modern playwright, parodies the title, suggesting that the letters should read "*I Now Represent Idi-*ots." Thus he vocalizes the modern contempt and the cynical attitude of our trendy, offbeat society for which nothing is sacred and Jesus holds no attraction.

147

Yet novelists and critics, however avant-garde and "with it," come and go. They have their day, burst like fireworks in the night sky, then they sputter out and are forgotten.

The cross of Jesus remains. Across 2,000 years it is still *God's signpost* pointing to His heart of love and mercy, "the hiding place of his power, and the inspiration of all Christian praise," as James Denney once called it.

Let Mark 15 bring us back to the cross. As we look at it the upraised figure of the crucified puts His spell upon us afresh, and we overcome two subtle temptations to which every Christian is exposed.

1. We sometimes imagine that this Good Friday drama is a well-worn theme and we know it so well. So it loses its wonder because of the deadening familiarity with which we treat it. We need to ponder and pray with Amy Carmichael:

God, hold us to that which
drew us first, when the Cross
was the only attraction, and we
wanted nothing else.

2. Equally pernicious is the idea that we as mature believers can outgrow the message of the cross. "Why," we may say, "the cross is for sinners, but we are advanced beyond that kindergarten stage. We need deep teaching!"

As though there could be any teaching deeper, more searching and more instructive than the story of Calvary! Every Christian needs constantly to pray:

Near the cross, O Lamb of God!
Bring its scenes before me;
Help me walk from day to day
With its shadow o'er me.

Fanny Crosby

How can we do these things? Let me make a couple of practical suggestions:

1. Read the chapter, with a conscious effort to understand it as though you were reading it *for the first time*.

2. Read it, asking how Jesus felt in it all, and this will evoke our gratitude and praise for all the pains, indignities, sufferings of soul that He bore. Above all, we will be thankful for His obedience unto death, and His action in dying

148

for us in the dreadful, unfathomable experience of separation from the Father. Especially we'll appreciate how His love shines through it all.

Here we survey that love
Which spoke in every breath,
Which crowned each action of His life,
And triumphed in His death.

Isaac Watts

3. Now read the story of Good Friday and try to see yourself in the men and women who pass across the stage: Pilate, the crowd, the Jewish leaders, Simon, the soldiers, Joseph, the women.

In the Tate Gallery in London, Stanley Spencer's painting, "Christ Carrying the Cross," hangs on display. When the men and women from the artist's village of Cookham came to see the painting, they observed one shattering feature nobody else spotted. Spencer had used *their* faces in the crowd scenes. There they were, painted into the mob who lined the road to Calvary and yelled, "Crucify!"

Maurice Collis, the artist's biographer, adds a comment: "The King of the World passes on His way to death. What an event that He should pass through Cookham."

And, through *your* street and city today!

Footnotes

1. More details along this line can be found in Ralph P. Martin, *Mark: Evangelist and Theologian*, pp. 65–69.

2. See Ralph P. Martin, *Mark: Evangelist and Theologian*, p. 178, for more discussion.

3. There is full discussion and defense of the Gospel's reference to Pilate's idea in J. Blinzler, *The Trial of Jesus*, and William L. Lane also comments on these matters.

4. Further details of Pilate's precarious situation are given in Ralph P. Martin, *New Testament Foundations*, Vol. 1, pp. 66–68.

5. Further information with line drawings of the victims' posture is given in J.H. Charlesworth's article, "Jesus and Jehohanan: An Archaeological Note on Crucifixion," *Expository Times*, 84, 1973, pp. 147–150, with the important conclusion: "It is not a confession of faith to affirm that Jesus died on Golgotha that Friday afternoon; it is a probability obtained by the highest canons of scientific historical research."

6. For the theology behind it, see L. Morris, *The Cross in the New Testament*, pp. 42–49.

7. See Ralph P. Martin, *Mark: Evangelist and Theologian*, pp. 183, 184, 213.

13

Every Day Is Easter

Mark 16:1-8

WHERE ARE WE GOING?

The women of the Gospel story were last at the cross (Mark 15:40–47) and they were first at the tomb. Three women are named standing at the cross in 15:40,41: Mary of Magdala (to distinguish her from several other women of that name). A second Mary is the mother of James and Joses. Salome was the wife of Zebedee and mother of the disciples, James and John (Matt. 27:56). Only two of these saw where Jesus was buried, in Mark 15:47, but the three women join forces on the day after the Sabbath to visit the tomb (16:1).

It is a striking fact that these faithful women play such a prominent role in discovering and announcing the resurrection. Today we accept it as natural, but for Jews who had then such a low opinion of a woman's status, especially in religious matters, this would have seemed shocking, even scandalous. But it is part of the scandal of the Gospel.

The Jewish idea that all women were not to be trusted as reliable witnesses reinforces the significance of the women's testimony. In fact, Jewish sources say that a woman is ineligible to give witness in a law court. From this point of view it would seem that the early Christians may well have been embarrassed by the fact that women first gave the news of Jesus' resurrection (see Luke 24:22). But it is surely a mark of authenticity that this is so, since no later group of Christians would have deliberately invented the story of women visiting the tomb and meeting the risen Lord (as in John 20:11–18), unless it happened just like that.

The timing of the women's visit to the grave site is given as "very early" in the morning, usually taken to be between 3 A.M.—6 A.M., but this is qualified in a typical Markan idiom (see Mark 1:35; 14:12) by "when the sun rose," i.e., at dawn. Possibly the second time-notice is added to deny the rumor that, as it was dark, the women may have gone to a grave other than the one in which Jesus was buried, and so they were mistaken in their conclusion that His grave was empty. Or else, there is a symbolism at work here: To the women the prophecy of Malachi 4:2 is made good, as "the Sun of righteousness" arises upon them "with healing in his wings."

The Christian affirmation, "Christ is alive," rests on a number of probative supports, as we can see from the New Testament records. None of those records would have been written in the first place if this conviction had been absent or doubted. The Church of the New Testament is the community of the resurrection. The living Lord was known, loved, served and obeyed as a present reality, which no one denied or doubted. Even the free-thinking Corinthians who were inclined to dispute the resurrection of believers (1 Cor. 15:12) never once cast a doubt on Christ's resurrection —a fact sometimes forgotten. Paul takes it for granted, and he builds on it as a common assumption.

151

Before we take a look at these few verses (Mark 16:1–8) and see the grounds for the resurrection confidence, we need to be aware that all modern editions of the New Testament show Mark's Gospel breaking off abruptly at 16:8. The last 12 verses printed in the *King James Version* are missing from the two oldest Greek manuscripts, and other important witnesses, including several church Fathers, Eusebius and Jerome, say that the passage was unknown in all copies of Mark to which they had access.

The consensus is moving in the direction of believing that Mark intended to bring his book to a close at verse 8, however abrupt that ending may seem to be. Also, the "fear" spoken of there is not one of uncertainty and foreboding about the future. It is rather the women's reaction to the presence of God and the awesome news that the Lord is risen and that they will see Him again.[1] So we must believe that, for whatever reason, Mark's Gospel ends at verse 8. Yet that is not the end of the story, as we shall see.[2]

WHAT DOES IT SAY?
The Empty Tomb

When the women who had noted carefully the place where the mangled corpse was laid to rest—in Joseph's grave (15:45,46)—decided to come back at the close of the Sabbath, they were in for a shock. The purpose of their visit was to anoint the body with spices which acted as a preservative—but their good intentions were to be thwarted. For one thing, in their agitation and excitement, they had forgotten that there was a large stone set as a barrier at the mouth of the cave.

Grave robbery and body snatching was a common occurrence among the Jews at this time, and the violation of graves resulting in the theft of corpses was a serious matter, punishable by Roman law.[3] Joseph (in Mark's Gospel) had taken this precaution against the removal of Christ's body (15:46).

To the women's amazement, the rock had been pushed over to one side, and the entrance to the grave was accessible. The grave, moreover, was open—but not exactly empty. Jesus was not there, but there was a "young man, dressed in a white robe, seated on the right side" (v. 5). Who this was is anybody's guess, and there have been several guesses, such as John Mark himself. Probably Mark intends us to understand that it was an angel (Acts 1:10), but it need not be so. What is more important is the word the youth spoke, "He is not here: see the place where they laid him." (v. 6, *RSV*).

The message of the young man inside the tomb also contains a mild reproof directed against the women. "You seek Jesus of Nazareth" (*RSV*). We remember that this verb, "seek," is always used by Mark in a bad sense—to seek Jesus either to place a temptation in His path (8:11–13) or else to turn Him aside from the way of God's will (1:37; 3:32). We might well suppose that the young man is accusing the women of failing to believe Jesus' promise that He would be raised. They have come to the wrong place to find Him. So the resurrection of Jesus is a mystery. No one saw Him rise, no one at least in the records of our Church Gospels. It remains for the noncanonical gospels to describe *how* He got out of the grave.[4]

And the grave was empty. In a way that we cannot understand, let alone explain, the body of Jesus had been moved. It had moved not simply from the grave slab to the outside world—which could have been done by various methods, such as if it were stolen, as Mary evidently thought possible according to John 20:13,15, or abducted by some disciples, as in the rumor of Matthew 28:13–15.[5]

The way in which the emptiness of the tomb could be explained away means that this line of conviction is none too strong as an apologetic argument. Paul never bases any conviction on it, though he is aware that Jesus was buried (1 Cor. 15:4) and His bodily resurrection therefore implies an empty grave.

The Appearances

Instead, Paul makes much of the various ways Jesus was seen after death (1 Cor. 15:5–8). The young man in Mark gives the invitation:

153

"He is not here. Look, the place where they laid
him . . . He is going before you into Galilee; there
you will see Him" (v. 7).

The appearances of the risen Lord are wide-ranging and
detailed, quite different in description from what would
have resulted if the stories had been made up. They are
characterized by diversity and variety in geographical loca-
tion. Each appearance has a purpose as He shows Himself
to men, women, groups, individuals and the like, at different times and in varying circumstances.[6]

These appearances are part of the fabric of Christian
apologetic. They are detailed and descriptive. He came to
His disciples in different places, at different times and for
different purposes (see Matt. 28:16–20; Luke 24:13–53;
John 20:11–29; 21:1–23; Acts 1:3–8; 9:3,4; 10:40–43; 22:17
–21; 26:12–18; Rev. 1:10–18).

The single common feature that runs through all this
narrative is that the reality of Jesus is known in a way that
inspired devotion, trust and obedience. However we may
want to "explain" the appearances and try to find a basis
for what the disciples saw in terms of controlled visions and
auditions, natural phenomena used by God, or even ESP,
the most important element is the objectivity of the appearances—there was something there or, better, someone
there, for them to see, and touch, and listen to (as Luke
says, Luke 24:39; and as John expressed so well, 1 John
1:1).[7]

The appearances were not self-invented nor were they
emotionally induced hallucinations. At the same time,
guided by Paul, we would want to say with certainty that
they were not simply ordinary happenings, as though Jesus
were seen after His resurrection as He was seen before it.

His body had been lifted to a new level of existence. It
was the same body yet different, as Paul explains in 1
Corinthians 15:40,44. Jesus' corpse had been laid to rest as
a physical body; it was raised as a spiritual body. That is,
a new body, still bearing resemblances to the old body, yet
fundamentally different, with new properties and powers

154

that made it suitable to the heavenly world. In Paul's terms again, a "body of humiliation" had been exchanged for a "body of glory" (Phil. 3:20,21).

A recent writer suggests helpfully a way of putting it: It was not the physical body of Jesus the Christians saw with their eyes, but it was with their physical eyes that they saw Jesus.[8] And that's what mattered.

Jesus' Promises

Mark puts most of his emphasis on this one fact: The youthful messenger recalled the promise of Jesus (made in 14:28) that, after death, He would meet His disciples again in Galilee (16:7). "As He told you" is a promise which clamps together the Jesus of the passion and the risen Lord of glory.

At His death, it was like a shepherd being killed and his flock dispersed. Now the shepherd comes back from the dead to seek out and lead forth the scattered sheep. "He is going before you" (16:7), as a shepherd who leads his flock (John 10:4).

This thought is found in Jewish writings where, at the end of the age, God will bring back the dispersed tribes of Israel and reunite them in the Kingdom. Jesus holds out this hope. To the "farewell" of the Upper Room He added the note of "au revoir," promising "I'll see you again." The heavenly messenger in 16:7 recalls this to the women, and bids them to tell the 11 disciples, that is the Twelve minus the lately deceased Judas, that Jesus will rendezvous with them in Galilee.

"In Galilee" is where it all began (1:14). Jesus opened His ministry there (1:28). There He called the Twelve and there He commissioned them. Now He is as good as His word, and He will meet them in familiar places.

But this time Galilee is a springboard of mission. He will send them out to do the task for which He prepared them long ago (3:14,15). In effect, it is to carry on the work—the ministry—He started and made possible by His death and victory. As the living Lord He is still with them in a way that has never been better described than in 16:20: "They went forth and preached everywhere, *the Lord working with them . . ."* (*RSV*, italics added).

Mark's Gospel is the Gospel of action. Jesus is the great Worker; as Teacher, Healer, Exorcist, Saviour. As the risen Lord, He bids all who read this Gospel to follow Him, and to know His friendship day by day.

WHAT DOES IT MEAN TODAY?

The story of the resurrection of Jesus is much more than a "happy ending" to a novel. It is richer even than the rewarding of Jesus for His obedience unto death. It is *the vindicating of who Jesus is.* Paul puts it crisply:

Jesus was "born of David's family in
 earthly descent,
(yet) declared to be the Son of God with power . . .
 by his resurrection from the dead" (Rom. 1:3,4).

So Mark's chapter puts the capstone on all that has gone before; all the claims Jesus has made, all the words He spoke about the Kingdom's presence and power, all His deeds of compassion and of love. In a word, His actions are now owned by God and shown to be of God. He is Lord, and as Lord, He has the authority given Him by His Father, to call men and women to follow Him and to continue His work in the world.

"Where the Action is" is where Jesus is; and where Jesus is at work, He summons us to share it with Him. But first we are invited to meet Him as living Lord.

Shakespeare is dust, and will not come
To question from his Avon tomb,
And Socrates and Shelley keep
An Attic and Italian sleep.

They see not. But, O Christians, who
Throng Holborn and Fifth Avenue,
May you not meet, in spite of death
A traveller from Nazareth?
 John Drinkwater

156

Footnotes

1. See William L. Lane, *Commentary*, pp. 590, 591.

2. The question of the text of Mark that breaks off at 16:8 with the words, "for they were afraid," is full of problems. See Ralph P. Martin, *New Testament Foundations*, vol. 1, pp. 217–220, for a survey of the evidence.

3. See E. Stauffer, *Jesus and His Story*, pp. 120, 121, 182, for an inscription discovered at Nazareth, to the effect of warning people against this crime.

4. In the apocryphal *Gospel of Peter* (early second century) we have an account of how the miracle occurred as the resurrection is described in some detail. The account of Jesus getting up out of the grave is printed in X. Léon-Dufour, *Resurrection and the Message of Easter*, pp. 270–272.

5. This objection was picked up by later Jewish objectors and answered by the Christian writer, Justin, in his *Dialogue with Trypho, a Jew*, ch. 108.

6. These are brought out in William Barclay's discussion, *Crucified and Crowned*, pp. 165–170.

7. See George E. Ladd, *I Believe in the Resurrection of Jesus*.

8. I owe this phrase to Dr. David R. Catchpole in an unpublished essay.

Bibliography

Alt, Albrecht. *Where Jesus Worked*. London: Epworth, 1961.

Anderson, Hugh. *The Gospel of Mark*. Greenville, S.C.: Attic, 1976.

Barclay, William. *Crucified and Crowned*. London: SCM, 1961.

Barrett, C.K. *Jesus and the Gospel Tradition*. London: SPCK, 1967.

Blinzler, J. *The Trial of Jesus*. Cork: The Mercer Press, 1959.

Bowker, John. *Jesus and the Pharisees*. Cambridge: University Press, 1974.

Charlesworth, J.H. "Jesus and Jehohanan: An Archaeological Note on Crucifixion." *Expository Times* 84, 1973, pp. 147–50.

Clow, W.M. *The Day of the Cross*. London: Hodder and Stoughton, 1909.

Cohn, Haim. *The Trial and Death of Jesus*. London: Weidenfeld and Nicolson, 1972.

Cullmann, Oscar. *Jesus and the Revolutionaries*. New York: Harper and Row, 1970.

Dodd, C.H. *The Founder of Christianity*. New York: Macmillan, 1970.

Findlay, J. Alexander. *Jesus As They Saw Him*. London: Epworth, 1921.

Hunter, A.M. *The Parables Then and Now*. Philadelphia: Westminster, 1971.

Jeremias, Joachim. *Infant Baptism in the First Four Centuries*. London: SCM, 1962.

_____. *Jesus' Promise to the Nations.* London: SCM, 1958.

_____. *New Testament Theology.* vol. 1. Philadelphia: Westminster, 1971.

_____. *The Parables of Jesus.* 2d ed. London: SCM, 1963.

Kallas, James. *Jesus and the Power of Satan.* Philadelphia: Westminster, 1968.

Kilpatrick, G.D. *The Trial of Jesus.* London: Dr. Williams' Library, 1953.

Ladd, George E. *I Believe in the Resurrection of Jesus.* Grand Rapids: Eerdmans, 1975.

Lane, William L. *Commentary on the Gospel of Mark.* Grand Rapids: Eerdmans, 1973.

Léon-Dufour, Xavier. *Resurrection and the Message of Easter.* New York: Holt, Rinehart and Winston, 1971.

Lightfoot, Robert H. *History and Interpretation in the Gospels.* London: Hodder and Stoughton, 1934.

Loos, H. van der. *The Miracles of Jesus.* Leiden: Brill, 1965.

Mally, E.J. "The Gospel According to Mark." *The Jerome Biblical Commentary.* London: Geoffrey Chapman, 1968.

Manson, T.W. article in *Studies in the Gospels.* Edited by D.E. Nineham. Naperville, IL: Allenson, 1955, p. 212.

_____. *The Beginning of the Gospel.* Cambridge: University Press, 1950.

_____. *The Sayings of Jesus.* London: SCM, 1949.

_____. *The Servant Messiah.* Cambridge: University Press, 1953.

_____. *The Teaching of Jesus.* Cambridge: University Press, 1931.

Martin, Ralph P. "Judas"; "Blasphemy"; "Idols, Meat Offered To." *New Bible Dictionary.* Edited by J.D. Douglas. Grand Rapids: Eerdmans, 1962.

_____. *Mark: Evangelist and Theologian.* Grand Rapids: Zondervan, 1973.

_____. *New Testament Foundations.* Vol. 1 Grand

Rapids: Eerdmans, 1975.

_____. *Worship in the Early Church*. Grand Rapids: Eerdmans, 1975.

Mauser, Ulrich W. *Christ in the Wilderness*. London: SCM, 1963.

Meye, Robert P. *Jesus and the Twelve*. Grand Rapids: Eerdmans, 1968.

Moore, A.L. *The Parousia in the New Testament*. Leiden: Brill, 1966.

Montefiore, Hugh. "Revolt in the Desert? Mark vi. 30ff." *New Testament Studies* 8, 1961, pp. 135–41.

Morris, Leon. *The Cross in the New Testament*. Grand Rapids: Eerdmans, 1965.

Orton, Joe. *Head to Toe*. London: Anthony Blond, 1970.

Rad, Gerhard von. *Theology of the Old Testament*. 2 vols. London: Lutterworth, 1962.

Rawlinson, A.E.J. *The Gospel According to St. Mark*. London: Methuen, 1925.

Richardson, Alan. *The Miracle Stories of the Gospels*. London: SCM, 1941.

Robinson, James M. *The Problem of History in Mark*. London: SCM Press, 1957.

Schweizer, Eduard. *Jesus*. Philadelphia: Westminster, 1971.

Sherwin-White, A.N. *Roman Society and Roman Law in the New Testament*. Oxford: Clarendon, 1963.

Shewell-Cooper, W.E. "Mustard." *The Zondervan Pictoral Encyclopedia of the Bible*. Vol. 4. Edited by M.C. Tenney. Grand Rapids: Zondervan, 1975, pp. 324f.

Stauffer, E. *Jesus and His Story*. London: SCM, 1960.

Strawson, W. *Jesus and the Future Life*. London: Epworth, 1961.

Taylor, Vincent. "Unsolved New Testament Problems: Apocalyptic Discourse of Mark 13." *Expository Times* 60, 1949, pp. 94–98.

_____. *The Gospel According to St. Mark*. London: Macmillan, 1959.

Trocmé, Etienne. *The Formation of the Gospel According to Mark*. Philadelphia: Westminster, 1975.